TWEETS
AND
CONSEQUENCES

60 Social Media Disasters in Politics and How You Can Avert a Career-Ending Mistake

MIKE SCHLOSSBERG

Published in the United States of America by Strategic Media Books,
Ind., 782 Wofford St., Rock Hill, SC 29730.
www.strategicmediabooks.com

Manufactured in the United States of America.

13-ISBN: 978-1939521-28-6
10-ISBN: 1-939521-28-9

Requests for permission should be directed to:
strategicmediabooks@gmail.com
or mailed to:
Permissions
Strategic Media Books, Inc.
782 Wofford St.
Rock Hill, SC 29730

Distributed to the trade by:
Cardinal Publishers Group
2402 North Shadeland Ave., Suite A
Indianapolis, IN 46219

To connect with the author, visit:
http://www.mikeschlossbergsocialmedia.com
http://www.facebook.com/MikeSchlossberg
http://www.twitter.com/MikeSchlossberg
And make sure to check out Mike's blog at
politicalfails.wordpress.com

To Mrs. Berger, Mrs. Stefanelli and Mrs. Rothbard,
my Middle School English teachers,
who taught me that writing can make worlds come alive.

Table of Contents

TWEETS AND CONSEQUENCES

INTRODUCTION

How to lose a career with just one click!

On May 27, 2011, the world of politics and social media changed forever when Anthony Weiner tweeted a picture of his boxer-covered genitalia to a 22-year-old college student. The subsequent scandal revealed that Weiner had engaged in this behavior with six to ten different women. Lacking support among his colleagues and facing a House ethics investigation, Weiner resigned in disgrace less than a month later.

Weiner would try to rehabilitate his career two years later by running for mayor of New York City. That, too, ended in disaster when further sexting scandals became public. Somehow, Weiner managed to eclipse the tawdriness of his previous episode when it came to light that he had used the Internet under the pseudonym "Carlos Danger." Danger had offered to buy 22-year-old Sydney Leathers an apartment in Chicago, all while sexting her and sending her naked pics. Weiner's mayoral campaign exploded in the most public manner possible: Weiner came in dead last in the race for mayor and has since slunk out of the political spotlight.

Weiner's story is a high visibility example of what happens when politicians and social media collide in the most negative way possible. Since social media first rose to worldwide prominence during the mid-2000s, there has been no shortage of hilarious and painful stories that detail how a person's moronic social media usage has cost them their job, career or worse. Examples include:

- Justice Sacco, the one-time executive for PR giant IAC, became a world-wide villain after tweeting, "Going to Africa. Hope I don't get AIDS. Just kidding. I'm white!" Sacco's relationship with IAC ended almost as soon as her plane touched the ground.

- Teacher Carly McKinney, who tweeted pictures of herself in various states of nudity and used social media to brag about how high she was and how she had drugs in her possession while despite the fact that she was in the parking lot of her school.

- Lindsey Stone, an employee of the non-profit LIFE, who uploaded a Facebook photo of herself on a work-related trip at Arlington Cemetery. In the photo, Stone is pictured pretending to yell and giving the middle finger next to a sign which reads "Silence and Respect." Stone was fired once the photos went public.

Horror stories aside, social media and politicians can, and usually do, go extremely well together. Appropriate social media use has accelerated the careers of countless individuals, including President Barack Obama, Senator Cory Booker (D-NJ) and Senator Chuck Grassley (R-IA). As of the start of 2014, more than 93 percent of the House of Representatives, along with 89 percent of the U.S. Senate, had an official presence on social media, with many members actively using social media personally. Governments have also figured out how to use the medium to better connect with their constituents. Many use social media to hold virtual Town Halls, distribute information, provide services and give emergency alerts.

Like gasoline to a fire, social media fuels a news story and makes it travel higher. Of course, elected officials and governments often find themselves on the negative end of a social media backlash. In the instances where a scandal doesn't actually originate on the internet, social media helps to carry the story far and wide. And in those instances when social media is, in fact, the primary arena for the destructive story... look out.

This book will provide an overview of what happens when politicians and governments using social media get it wrong: What mistakes were made, what corrective action was taken, and what we can learn from their screw-ups. The book is broken down into sections and chapters, categorized by the specific type of error that was made. Exact categorization is impossible, as there is incredible overlap. For example, it's difficult to argue that a tweet which invokes stereotypes or violence isn't also a failure of intelligence or judgment. Other chapters include stories on posts that were accidentally sent to the wrong account, sex, brands and politics, absurdly stupid technical mistakes, and intentionally malicious social media use.

Each story will follow the same format. First, it will lay out the background behind each blooper, providing context and explaining what led up to the mistake committed. It will then review the actual mistake, phrased as "the fail," complete with pictures, tweets, screen-grabs and other relevant media. It will then discuss the response and consequences of each fail, detailing what went well in the reaction phase and what didn't. Consequences will also be examined, including media reaction, relevant quotes from other officials and the long-term ramifications for the individual, campaign or governments involved. Last, each chapter will discuss the lesson, reviewing what the reader can learn from each mistake.

The goal of this book, to some extent, is to make you laugh. Human stupidity is almost always funny. However, it can also be incredibly depressing, particularly if you have a bone of empathy in your body. Sure, some of these politicians got what they deserved. But many made innocent mistakes or had a momentary lapse in judgment that resulted in a ruined career and shattered life. As such, though we're trying to entertain, the real purpose of this book is to teach. Politicians make mistakes, but the real question is this: How can you avoid making the same ones?

SECTION I

Dumb, Dumb, Dumb

Social media shows off a lack of intelligence or judgment

It has been said repeatedly that elected officials are simply reflections of the people that elect them. After reading the stories below, you will probably pray that this isn't the case. The twenty-one stories in this section will lay out examples of elected officials and organizations that have used social media to do incredibly stupid things that will seriously call into question their judgment and character. Each story has its own specific lesson, but as a general rule, you probably don't want to ever do anything that any of these people did. Avoid repeating their mistakes at all costs!

૪ ෮

Chapter One:

The Senator that wasn't

The Background: In 2010, at the height of the power of the Tea Party in American politics, conservative attorney Joseph Miller challenged incumbent Senator Lisa Murkowski for the Republican nomination for the U.S. Senate. Miller charged that Murkowski, a moderate Republican, was far too liberal for the State. After spending more than $100,000 of his own money, Miller stunned the political world by beating Murkowski by 1,630 votes. Given Alaska's Republican-friendly environment, it was widely assumed that Miller would win the general election. Murkowski, unwilling to accept defeat, announced in September that she would run a write-in campaign for the Senate. The last successful write-in candidate for the U.S. Senate was in 1956, when Senator Strom Thurmond pulled off the feat.

The Fail: With barely a month to go before the midterm elections, Joe Miller went to Washington, D.C. and he tweeted about it:

Think I'll do some house hunting while I'm in DC #teaparty #tcot #tpp #alaska #ak

Guess I should pick out some office furniture, as well, while in DC #teaparty #tcot #tpp #alaska #ak

Then there's the matter of a name plaque for the door #teaparty #tcot #tpp #alaska #ak

My sincere appreciation for the warm welcome, including from future colleagues in DC #teaparty #tcot #tpp #alaska #ak

This wasn't Miller's only run-in with Twitter. About six weeks prior to the above tweets, Miller compared Senator Murkowski to a prostitute:

What's the difference between selling out your party's values and the oldest profession? http://bit.ly/93kXBr #teaparty #tcot #alaska #ak

The Response and Consequences: Any candidate knows that you never, ever declare victory until the votes have been counted. And that is definitely not done in a competitive race, when you have two opponents, a month before the election. Miller deleted the tweets after being sent, but it was far too late. Murkowski jumped on Miller's arrogance, calling the tweets "hubris." In response, Miller claimed that the tweets had been sent by a campaign volunteer who had access to the Twitter account.

In addition to the house-hunting and whore-comparing tweets, Miller's campaign faced additional controversies. In October 2010, private security guards handcuffed a journalist at a Miller event. Prior to running for office, Miller was found to have used government computers for political purposes in 2008; these stories came to light in late October. The tweets, journalist arrest and Miller's reluctance to answer questions about his prior work history damaged his campaign. On Election Day, Murkowski pulled in 41 percent of the vote. Miller earned 34 percent, while Democrat Scott McAdams earned 24 percent.

Miller refused to accept the results of the race and challenged Murkowski's victory in federal court, alleging that the State of Alaska was using an unconstitutional standard to count the votes. After weeks of court proceedings and multiple appeals, Miller finally conceded on December 31.

The Lesson:

- Control over social media: If Miller's campaign truly allowed a volunteer to tweet on behalf of the candidate, it was a colossal blunder. At the national level of politics, only paid professionals should have social media access. Giving the same to a volunteer is the equivalent of giving a fourteen year old a Mustang, a fifth of Jack, the keys, and a pat on the back. A volunteer can be allowed control of social media at a more local level, but even then, strict guidelines must be placed so the volunteer knows what to tweet.

- Credibility matters: If these tweets were the first time in which Miller had a run-in with the media that showed poor judgment, the results may not have been as catastrophic. But, the multiple bad tweets, handcuffing of a journalist (not a preferred tactic for dealing with the media) and refusal to answer questions about his past (fair game in campaigns, particularly when it deals with a candidate's professional life) all helped to fuel a perception that Miller was arrogant, irrational and not ready for prime time.

- Hide your arrogance: Arrogance leads to colossal blunders in politics, and it gets even worse when you let your prospective constituents know that you think you are winning. Voters want candidates to earn their vote and they don't appreciate when a candidate takes their victory for granted. Candidates must always run like they are thirty points behind and never, ever give the impression that they think victory is assured.

Chapter Two:

The NRA goes on auto-pilot – at a bad, bad moment

The Background: On July 20, 2012, James Holmes opened fire at a sold-out screening of *The Dark Knight Rises*. Armed with multiple weapons, tear gas grenades and a load-bearing vest, Holmes killed 12 and injured 70 before being arrested in the parking lot of the theater. The nation reacted with sadness, grief, shock and anger. As has become part of the national dialogue when these tragedies occur, many quickly wondered what impact the shooting would have on the national gun control debate.

The Fail: Nine hours after the shooting, the Twitter account of the NRA's official journal, *American Rifleman*, tweeted out the following:

> Good morning, shooters. Happy Friday! Weekend plans?

The Response and Consequences: The tweet was deleted two hours after being sent. When contacted by a news agency, an NRA spokesperson appeared unfamiliar of the tweet. The NRA would later claim that the tweet was sent out by an individual who was unaware of the tragedy of Colorado, and that the tweet was being taken completely out of context. Many hypothesized that the tweet had been scheduled to be sent before the shooting. The tweet was sent via HootSuite, a social media management platform that allows for tweets to be scheduled ahead of time. It was thus likely that the tweet had been scheduled to be sent before the shooting took place. Additionally, the tweet was sent at 9:20am, and Hootsuite only allows for tweets to be scheduled at times that end in 0 or 5.

The Twitter account was deleted a week after the shooting, but was later restored. As of April 2014, it has over 64,000 followers.

The Lesson:

- Careful with scheduling: Some advocate that social media users don't use a scheduling platform, such as Hootsuite. If you run multiple accounts or are short on time, a social media management platform is virtually a requirement. That being said, users shouldn't confuse Hootsuite with auto-pilot; the person responsible for scheduling tweets still has to remain plugged into the world and alter the social media schedule if local or world events dictate.

- Quick response: The tweet itself was bad. But, to their credit, the NRA got rid of it in under two hours. They also had a quick explanation about what happened, although that explanation didn't filter to the first spokesman contacted by reporters. Mistakes are unavoidable, but how you handle the aftermath can be critical. For example, imagine how much the fallout from this insensitive post would have been enhanced if the NRA's response had not had an implicit acknowledgment that the tweet was inappropriate.

Chapter Three:

A Facebook rant from the mayor of the United States' 61st biggest city

The Background: On September 1, 2006, Pittsburgh Mayor Bob O'Connor died of lymphoma. He was succeeded by Luke Ravenstahl, President of the City Council. At 26, Ravenstahl was the youngest mayor in Pittsburgh's history. Ravenstahl was subsequently elected to his own term in 2007 and reelected in 2009, but questions emerged about his judgment and maturity. Among those allegations were his participation in a free golf tournament held by an organization that Ravenstahl was trying to exempt from paying some taxes and his use of a police vehicle to attend a concert. In 2013, in the middle of a hotly contested primary, Ravenstahl announced that he was withdrawing from the race, citing the grueling demands of the job on himself and his family. At the time, the Pittsburgh Police Department was under FBI investigation for allegations that public resources were improperly spent on the mayor and hidden from public view.

The Fail: Ravenstahl had a notoriously bad relationship with the *Pittsburgh Post-Gazette*, one of Pittsburgh's daily papers. Despite withdrawing from the mayor's race, Ravenstahl continued to stay involved in the election and was the chairman of a group that was attacking Councilman Bill Peduto, a political nemesis of Ravenstahl and candidate for mayor. Using his personal Facebook profile, Ravenstahl launched into a rambling, grammatically incorrect Facebook rant after the *Pittsburgh Post-Gazette* ran an article that tied him to the group attacking Councilman Peduto:

> Breaking news: One of America's (self-proclaimed) greatest newspapers actually takes the time to pull the records of an account that's been in existence for years! Congrats to [reporter] Tim McNulty and the tremendous work of the entire team from [executive editor] David Shribman on down. You really blew the cover off of this one. Yawn... Truth is no one is hiding anything, nor has attempted to. I have personally been the Chairman of this committee since its inception. In fact, its Chairman and intentions are much more transparent than your rag of a newspaper. At least I'm honest and truthful about my support and don't attempt to hide behind a mantel of a "newspaper". It's actually laughable to think that you print your newspaper every day with a straight face. It doesn't take much to see who the P-G supports and doesn't

support. – Back to that in a minute... I was honored to receive the tremendous financial support from hundreds of donors who believe in all of the wonderful things happening in our city. They (and I) want to see that continue. The effort is based on that – and that alone. It's 100% factual and begins to expose the real Bill Peduto. Future ads will do the same. Finally – I love how the "haters" love to preach about the law and following it..... Except of course... When it doesn't benefit th! The facts are that this is legal in every sense of the law and nothing more than a committee expressing its first amendment rights. You 14th warders love that, right? Anyway – back to the P-G bias... The only question that remains is whether the P-G will endorse Peduto this Sunday or next. Curious about your thoughts... My guess is this Sunday – gives their man two whole weeks to talk about it!

The Response and Consequences: Ravenstahl never publically commented on the bizarre rant. The fallout against Ravenstahl was limited; sure, newspaper columnists blasted him, but Ravenstahl had already withdrawn from his reelection race. However, the Facebook comment did nothing to help the impression, held by some, that the mayor was an immature, irrational politician who had ascended to a position for which he was not ready. To top it off, Bill Peduto won anyway, nabbing a solid 52 percent of the vote in a four-way primary and beating his nearest opponent by 12 percent.

The Lesson:

- Never, ever leave a comment in an online newspaper article: Want to comment on a newspaper article? Don't. Stop it now. No elected official should ever leave a comment in an online article. To do so brings you down to the level of those who you are supposed to be better than. No good can come from an online comment, though a lot of bad can. If you do write online, check your grammar and spelling. Nothing says, "I'm ill-prepared to be the mayor of the second largest city in Pennsylvania" stronger than a Facebook rant with poor grammar and spelling.

Chapter Four:

The Councilman who posted bestiality pics to Facebook... while making an anti-gay statement?

The Background: Henry Davis, Jr. is a Democratic member of Common Council for South Bend, Indiana. Davis was no stranger to controversy: in October 2012, Davis Jr. was detained while his father was arrested following a traffic stop in South Bend. As a member of Common Council, Davis was viewed as opposing gay rights, having twice voted against adding sexual orientation and gender identity to the city's human rights ordinance.

The Fail: In a January 2013 Facebook post, Davis decided to make a statement against the repeal of "Don't Ask, Don't Tell," the U.S. military's former rules regarding homosexual troops being able to openly serve. Davis did so by linking homosexuality and bestiality. As noted by local media, Davis posted an "explicit photograph of a man and a dog... along with a link to a blog post criticizing the repeal of "Don't Ask,

Don't Tell." The blog itself took viewers to reunionblackfamily.com, which, among other posts, had entries headlined "Whites used black babies as alligator bait" and "White NYPD cops rejoice after beating up black teen after botched stop and frisk."

The Response and Consequences: The criticism of Davis on his own Facebook page was almost immediate, and Davis pulled down the pic and gave a half-hearted apology: "I regret that an article posted to my Facebook page was mistakenly taken as an expression of my personal or political views."

The statement did little to calm the public's anger against Davis, and a slew of public outcry quickly followed. Eight residents filed a public complaint against Davis, saying that, "The posting on Facebook is obscene, against public decency and shows a total lack of professionalism." The written complaint was forwarded to Common Council's Rules Committee, which is made up of three council members. The committee could have recommended a wide array of possible sanctions, up to and including removal from office. Meanwhile, the St. Joseph County Prosecutor's Office announced that it was seeking the appointment of a special prosecutor to investigate citizen complaints against Davis that were related to the original Facebook post.

A few days after Davis' first apology, he was forced to issue a second, more comprehensive one. At a press conference where he was joined by his wife and pastor, Davis said, "Many people have found it offensive. It was a mistake on my part and for that I

am truly remorseful and I ask for your forgiveness."
At the press conference, Davis also made the claim
that he had never actually seen the picture himself.

Ultimately, Councilman Davis was lucky. South
Bend's Rules Committee recommended a six month
censure, during which time Davis would not be
allowed to chair any committee. If the motion was
accepted, Davis would have remained a voting
member of South Bend Council. However, ultimately,
no punishment stuck: the recommendation of the
Rules Committee did not receive a majority vote, and
was dismissed.

The Lesson:

- Some content is – and needs to be –
  completely off-limits: If you think using
  Facebook to post a pornographic picture of
  a man having a sex with a dog is
  appropriate, then not only are you not cut
  out for politics, but you clearly have more
  serious judgment issues that you need to
  work on. The fact that Davis made this
  post in connection to an argument against
  the repeal of "Don't Ask, Don't Tell" makes
  the post even more offensive: he was
  essentially tying together homosexuality
  and bestiality, two subjects that most
  Americans can agree have nothing to do
  with each other. Davis should never have
  posted such offensive content to his
  Facebook page.

- What you post will be assumed to be your beliefs: One of the more interesting claims here is that Davis said he only posted the picture in an effort to start a conversation. Giving Davis the benefit of the doubt for a moment and assuming that this claim is true, this incident illuminates a very important point: if you share content via your social media platforms, you are ultimately going to be held responsible for it. More to the point, the content you share, unless you explicitly profess otherwise, will be assumed to be reflective of who you are.

Chapter Five:

I wasn't sexting my lover, I was tweeting my daughter.

The Background: Elected in 2006, Congressman Steve Cohen (D-TN) serves in Tennessee's 9th District. Cohen has never been shy from appearing in media that more traditional congressmen shun, including *The Colbert Report, The Young Turks* and *Conspiracy Theory*, hosted by none other than Jesse "The Body" Ventura, the former governor of Minnesota. No stranger to controversy, Cohen got into hot water when he compared Republican attempts to repeal Obamacare to Nazi propaganda master Joseph Goebbels. Cohen had also found himself on the bad end of publicity as a result of his Twitter account. In April 2013, Cohen attended a Cyndi Lauper concert, then tweeted Lauper: "@cyndilauper great night, couldn't believe how hot u were.see you again next Tuesday.try a little tenderness."

The Fail: During the 2013 State of the Union, Steve Cohen sent out the following tweets to model Victoria Brink:

@victoria_brinkpleased u r watching. ilu

@victoria_brink nice to know you were watchin SOTU(state of the union). Happy Valentines beautiful girl. ilu

The Response and Consequences: At first, it appeared that Cohen had been caught sending a gorgeous blond model creepy tweets. Had he accidentally sent a public reply, instead of a direct message, a la Anthony Weiner? Well, yes, but it wasn't what it looked like. In a press conference the day after the State of the Union, Cohen revealed that Brink wasn't his lover; she was, in fact, his daughter, whom Cohen had learned about only three years prior. The press conference was the first time that Cohen publicly acknowledged the relationship. Unfortunately, as Cohen would learn three months later, his assertion of paternity was wrong: a DNA test would conclude that Cohen was not Brink's father; that man was John Brink.

The Lesson:

- Careful with the @ and DM: This scandal, like the Anthony Weiner scandal, may never have gone public had Cohen just double-checked what button on his phone he had clicked. This is a common mistake, but Cohen's situation serves as a reminder that Twitter users must be careful with what they press.

- Trust but verify: This is a bit of a more general piece of advice, but never go public with any information before you know it to be true. When Cohen said that Brink was his daughter, it was February. A DNA test was conducted in late May. In other words, Cohen told the world that he had a daughter when he had no concrete proof. This is not a position anyone should ever put themselves in.

Chapter Six:

A Level 85 Orc for Senate

The Background: In 2012, Colleen Lachowicz (D) challenged incumbent Senator Tom Martin (R-25) for the Maine State Senate. For the prior twenty-five years, Lachowicz worked as a social worker. In her spare time, Lachowicz was an avid World of Warcraft player. World of Warcraft is an online fantasy game in which players can become characters that play with others from across the world. Individuals can complete quests, engage in player-to-player combat and level-up in an all-immersive environment. Lachowicz also was a frequent commenter in World of Warcraft online forums.

The Fail: To the surprise of many, including Tom Martin, the Maine Republican Party sent out this attack ad against Lachowicz:

The mailer criticized Lachowicz on two fronts. First, it criticized her for being immersed in a fantasy world that looks very strange to non-players. Second, it reprinted her comments in online forums, which included vulgarity, bragging about losing productivity at her job thanks to Warcraft, and violent comments.

The Response and Consequences: Lachowicz refused to apologize for her time spent on World of Warcraft, though she didn't directly address her use of curse words and boastful comments about her laziness. Said Lachowicz, "I think it's weird that I'm being targeted for playing online games. Apparently I'm in good company since there are 183 million other Americans who also enjoy online games. What's next? Will I be ostracized for playing Angry Birds or Words with Friends? If so, guilty as charged!"

Tom Martin claimed ignorance on the attacks, saying that they were being coordinated by the Republican Party, not his campaign.

Both Lachowicz and Martin had enrolled in Maine's Clean Election Act, a voluntary program in which both received public financing, thus dramatically limiting the amount of private donations they could receive. Unable to donate directly to her campaign, gamers created a separate PAC under which they could raise money for Lachowicz, ultimately raising more than $6,300. The Maine Republican Party fired back, claiming that by posting on the ActBlue page and encouraging others to visit the donation pages, Lachowicz was violating the Clean Elections Act. However, in a 5-0 ruling, the Maine Ethics Commission cleared Lachowicz of any wrongdoing.

Ultimately, the story went international and was featured in multiple news outlets, including the *Chicago Tribune, Time Magazine, Slate, Politico and Kotaku*.

As for the election? Lachowicz won anyway. She defeated Martin by a 8,666-7,753 margin.

The Lesson:

- Online lasts forever: Lachowicz clearly said things that she probably never would have if she knew she was ever going to run for public office. That being said, everyone, politician or not, needs to be careful with what they post online. Furthermore, if you know you have content online that you know you shouldn't, try to get it removed ASAP.

- Online doesn't always matter: The attacks were different, to say the least. However, they ultimately didn't affect the outcome of the election. Online behavior has to be a little more radical than someone playing World of Warcraft to make an impact in a campaign. Had Republicans chosen to focus on Lachowicz's online comments about her laziness, instead of confusing the message with her World of Warcraft play, they might have been more effective.

- Don't anger a sleeping giant: In this case, the gaming community rallied around Lachowicz, setting up separate PACs and raising money on her behalf. Sure, negative ads may be necessary in a political campaign, but they can boomerang by causing others to engage that may never have been involved otherwise. In this case, $6,300 was directly raised on Lachowicz's behalf as a result of these attacks.

Chapter Seven:

Refudiate

The Background: Park 51, better known as the "Ground Zero Mosque," was the proposed construction of an Islamic Center two blocks from the former World Trade Center site in New York. Unveiled in 2010, the building was set to be used as a community center, complete with an auditorium, theatre, performing arts center, prayer space, athletic facilities, childcare services, Halal food court and more. A controversy erupted shortly thereafter, with many arguing that it was inappropriate for a "mosque" to open so close to the World Trade Center.

The Fail: On July 18, 2010, former Alaska governor and vice presidential candidate Sarah Palin waded into the controversy with this tweet:

Ground Zero Mosque supporters: doesn't it stab you in the heart, as it does ours throughout the heartland? Peaceful Muslims, pls refudiate

The problem? Refudiate isn't a word. Palin combined "refute" and "repudiate."

The Response and Consequences: National media quickly picked up on the errant tweet, and Palin found herself on the receiving end of significant scorn. Huffington Post referred to the tweet as a gaffe, while ABC news noted that the tweet was deleted hours after it was sent. Palin, however, tweeted a typical unrepentant follow-up:

> "Refudiate," "misunderestimate," "wee-wee'd up." English is a living language. Shakespeare liked to coin new words too. Got to celebrate it!

Palin would later say that refudiate was a typo: "I pressed an F instead of a P and peopled freaked out. Make lemonade out of lemons! "However, four days before the tweet, Palin appeared on Fox News, where she used refudiate in a televised interview.

Palin was honored by at least one organization for her tweet: New Oxford American Dictionary named refudiate the 2010 Word of the Year. Said the dictionary's editors: "... we have concluded that neither 'refute' nor 'repudiate' seems consistently precise, and that 'refudiate' more or less stands on its own, suggesting a general sense of 'reject.'"

The Lesson:

- Check your spelling and your grammar: If Palin had waited ten seconds to double check her tweet before hitting send, she might have caught the mistake.

If you are going to wade into a controversy, use proper English: Of course, politicians constantly wade into controversial issues; that's their job. Indeed, Palin was the latest in a series of conservative political figures who called for the cancellation of the Park51 project. However, making up words does nothing to help your cause. Instead, it detracts from the seriousness of whatever issue you are discussing. Palin probably did her side more harm than good by bringing a distraction to the matter. Words clearly matter.

Chapter Eight:

Honoring Sandy Hook victims via ammunition distribution

The Background: December 14, 2013, marked the one-year anniversary of one of the most disturbing days in American history. On that date in 2012, Adam Lanza killed twenty first-graders and six adults at Sandy Hook Elementary School in Newtown, Connecticut. As the anniversary of the tragedy approached, communities throughout America pulled together to honor the victims of the massacre. One such event was "26 Random Acts of Kindness," which sought to honor Sandy Hook's dead by encouraging participants to engage in random acts of kindness.

At around this same time, 26-year-old Greg Beck unseated an incumbent and was elected to the School Board of Brookfield, Connecticut. Brookfield directly borders Newtown.

The Fail: In response to a Facebook post promoting "26 Random Acts of Kindness," Beck posted this comment:

I shall buy my friends who are gun enthusiasts
a box of ammunition on days 1-26

The Response and Consequences: The reaction, of course, was overwhelmingly negative against Beck, and calls for him to resign began almost immediately. In the immediate aftermath of the post, Beck issued a statement apologizing, saying, "The comments were insensitive and completely indefensible. I acknowledge the damage this has caused and truly had no malicious intentions. Nor were there any attempts on my part to downplay the Sandy Hook Tragedy behind the comment."

Beck made it through two public meetings without resigning; however, at both of those meetings, most of the public comment period was dominated by angry residents who demanded Beck's resignation. By the time the third public meeting rolled around, Beck had enough, and resigned shortly before the meeting was set to begin.

However, the story didn't end here. Beck made the posts while at work as an emergency dispatcher, which is a publicly funded job. Two citizens made ethics complaints against Beck, and if Beck had been found guilty, he could have been removed from his position. However, the Board of Ethics found that the complaints could only be made against Beck if he were a public official, and Beck had resigned at this point. As such, the complaints were tossed, and Beck escaped without any further consequences... besides the national humiliation he had endured for his poor judgment.

The Lesson:

- Don't say some things: Don't talk about violence. Don't talk about guns unless you are discussing hunting, hobbies or self-defense, and even then, be prepared for some angry responses. And never, ever talk about guns in a caviler way when referring to one of the most emotionally scaring episodes of gun violence that this country has ever known.

- Watch where you are posting from: The content of Beck's post was bad enough, but the fact that he posted it while at work, as an emergency dispatcher, made a bad situation even worse. Beck is fortunate that he didn't lose his job, and this incident highlighted a critical truth of Social Media: when and from where you post something can often be as bad as the content of a post itself.

Chapter Nine:

Stay away from message boards

The Background: Mike Maggio is an Arkansas judge, serving in the 20th Judicial Circuit of the State. In early 2014, Judge Maggio kicked off a campaign to run for the Arkansas Court of Appeals. As a judge, Maggio heard a variety of hearings, including on adoption proceedings. These types of hearings are supposed to remain confidential.

The Fail: In March of 2014, the Blue Hog Report first reported an astounding breach of confidentiality and ethics. It alleged that Judge Maggio had made a variety of deeply offensive posts on the TigerDroppings.com, a message board for fans of Louisiana State University. Blue Hog Report also alleged that Maggio used the board to discuss details of the adoption hearings of actress Charlize Theron. That information was supposed to remain confidential.

Maggio made the posts under the username "geauxjudge." Among his comments:

- If your name sounds black, your future is not bright: "How many Doctors do you hear named Dr. Taneesha or HaHa? How many bankers do you hear named Brylee?"

- Men have two needs from women: "Feed me and f*<k me."

- Homosexual sex is "just a small step" from bestiality.

Additionally, Maggio posted that he had "a friend who is the judge that did her [Charlize Theron's] adoption today" and discussed how Theron attended court camouflaged, in order to disguise her appearance from the press. When asked by another poster if it was a black baby, Maggio replied, "Yep."

The Response and Consequences: With evidence mounting against him, Maggio was forced to admit that he was geauxjudge. In a statement, Maggio said, "I take full responsibility for the comments that have been attributed to me. I apologize deeply for my lapse in personal judgment and for that, I have no excuse. The comments posted were not acceptable. These comments are not reflective of who I am." Maggio also announced that he was withdrawing from his race for Arkansas Court of Appeals.

This story appeared across the United States, but also appeared in England's *Daily Mail*, giving Maggio international infamy.

Rules of Judicial Ethics require that a Judge act "in a manner that promotes public confidence in the independence, integrity, and impartiality of the judiciary, and shall avoid impropriety and the appearance of impropriety." As a result, the Arkansas Judicial Discipline and Disability Commission announced that it was investigating Maggio's remarks. The commission has the power to impose sanctions on Maggio, including removal from office. Less than three weeks after the story first broke, the Arkansas Supreme Court issued a two-page ruling that reassigned all of Maggio's cases to other courts.

Ultimately, the message board scandal ended Maggio's career as a judge. The Arkansas Judicial Discipline and Disability Commission found that Maggio's comments gave "rise to legitimate concerns that bias would overcome fairness and due process for a large number of potential litigants and their attorneys." As such, the Commission suspended Maggio for the rest of his judicial term and banned him from ever holding another judicial office again, noting that his comments made him "unfit for the bench."

This wasn't Judge Maggio's only brush with ethics complaints. At the same time that this scandal broke, Maggio was under investigation for receiving a financial contribution from the owner of the Greenbrier Nursing and Rehabilitation Center. Days after receiving such a contribution, a Maggio ruling reduced a financial award against Greenbrier from $5.2 million to $1 million. In June 2014, Judge Maggio appeared before the Arkansas Ethics Commission. The hearing itself was confidential and Maggio refused to comment on the matter; however, less than two weeks after the hearing, Maggio settled the campaign finance violation of the case, accepting a $750 fine for taking campaign donations about state limits.

The Lesson:

- Respect confidentiality: Under no circumstances should you ever make post (even if you think they are being made "anonymously") that violates ethical or legal confidentiality rules. As a judge, Maggio should have known better.

- There is no anonymity: You should never mistake not using your identity on the internet with being anonymous. As the post above showed, no one is so smart that they cannot get caught making "anonymous" postings. IP addresses, off-hand comments, language usage and any number of other factors can ultimately result in an anonymous user being exposed. There is never a need to make anonymous comments – it is simply not worth the risk.

Chapter Ten:

Aren't X-rays of dead people funny?

The Background: Dr. Milton Wolf is a Kansas radiologist and distant cousin to President Barack Obama. In 2013, Wolf announced that he would challenge three-term Kansas Senator Pat Roberts in the Republican Primary. Wolf alleged that Roberts was insufficiently conservative for Kansas voters and that he was disconnected from his home state. Wolf's charges were boosted when it was reported that Senator Roberts was registered to vote at a home of two of his donors, and that Roberts rarely stayed at the residence. The residency questions helped to drop Roberts' favorability numbers, and in 2014, it appeared that Wolf's campaign was gaining real momentum.

The Fail: In February 2014, the *Topeka Capitol-Journal* reported that Wolf had posted pictures of X-rays to Facebook, complete with ghoulish commentary mocking the dead and the tragedies that had befallen them. Among the posts:

- A high-resolution X-ray of a man who had been shot in the temple and killed, complete with images of the man's shattered skull and bullet fragments. When questioned about the positioning of the man's head, Wolf responded, "Sheesh...it's not like the patient was going to complain."

- An image of a person whose head resembled a "smashed pumpkin" after a gunshot. In response to the carnage wrought by the gun, Wolf wrote, "One of my all-time favorites. From my residency days there was a pretty active 'knife and gun club' at Truman Medical Center. What kind of gun blows somebody's head completely off? I've got to get one of those... It reminds (me) of the scene from 'Terminator 2' when they shoot the liquid metal terminator guy in the face at close range and it kind of splits him open temporarily almost like a flower blooming. We all find beauty in different things."

The Response and Consequences: Ethics experts agreed that Wolf's posts were questionable at best. John Carney, president of the Center for Practical Bioethics: "The dignity and privacy of the individual should be protected. It doesn't sound like they're being protected if they're, obviously, on Facebook." Carney also called the postings, "beyond alarming for a professional in the field of medicine." Jerry Slaughter, President of the Kansas Medical Society, noted that, "Absent any legitimate educational purpose of context, this is not ethical behavior."

When initially confronted by the *Topeka Capitol-Journal*, Wolf said that he made these posts to show that there are "real consequences to some of the evil out there in the world." Later, he asked a reporter for copies of the Facebook posts in question. When denied, Wolf walked away from the reporter, saying, "I'm not going to play these kind of gotcha games."

In his initial campaign statement, Wolf accused the Roberts campaign of "readying a war on doctors" and said that Senator Roberts had "planted stories in the media designed to mislead voters about Dr. Wolf." The statement, however, contained no apology or statement of regret. That changed the next day, when Roberts made a second statement, saying, "Several years ago I made some comments about a few of these X-ray images that were insensitive to the seriousness of what the x-ray images revealed. Soon thereafter, I removed those X-ray images and comments, again several years ago. For them to be published in a much more public context now, by a political adversary who would rather declare war on doctors than answer serious questions that Kansans have, is truly sad. However, my mistakes are my own and I take full responsibility for them... To those who I have offended, I am truly sorry and I ask your forgiveness."

Senator Roberts and his allies, of course, attacked Wolf's Facebook posts. Brad Dayspring, spokesman for the National Republican Senate Committee, accused

Wolf of engaging in "freakish behavior," saying, "Wolf is now embroiled in serious ethical and legal questions and challenges, effectively destroying any small hope that he had for a serious campaign."

The entire episode would ultimately become a leading criticism against Wolf, and it was successful: Senator Roberts held on and defeated Wolf in the August 2014 primary, winning by a 48-41 percent margin, with two other candidates picking up the remainder of the votes.

The Lesson:

- Respect confidentiality: Since there was no identifying information available in any of the X-rays posted, Wolf may not have violated any laws. However, while he might be legally covered, the posts were ethically and morally repugnant. Wolf never should have made such silly and immature posts. Social media users should always err on the side of confidentiality when it comes to their posts, particularly for something as significant as the demise of another human being.

- Don't be glib: This applies to all types of situations in politics: never be glib. Glib, sarcastic and dismissive attitudes are a recipe for disaster in politics. That potential is significantly multiplied when you note that Wolf's glibness was in reference to the violent deaths of multiple individuals. Some attitudes should not be used in politics. Glibness is one of them.

Chapter Eleven:

Congressman on Intelligence Committee uses Twitter to reveal previously embargoed trip to Iraq

The Background: In 2009, American troops were actively engaged in the Iraqi War. Politicians of all stripes were constantly in the area, visiting troops and touring facilities. Such trips were under high security and usually kept secret until their completion.

The Fail: In February of 2009, Congressman Peter Hoekstra (R-MI) was among a delegation of American officials that visited the war-torn country. At the time, the Congressman was a member of the House Intelligence Committee. The trip was supposed to have been embargoed until it was over, meaning that while some knew about the trip, no one was reporting it in the media. This was, at the time, standard operating procedure for such trips, designed to protect the safety and security of dignitaries. However, in a series of tweets, Hoekstra discussed the trip and his general location, live from Iraq:

On the way to Andrews Air Force base. 12 hour flight to mid-east Be back on Mon instead of Tues. Votes mon. I'll keep you posted.

Just landed in Baghdad. I believe it may be the first time I've had bb service in Iraq. 11th trip here.

Moved into green zone by helicopter Iraqi flag now over palace. Headed to new U.S. embassy. Appears calmer less chaotic than previous here.

Iraq! Issues! Long term impact on containing Iran. Need a coherent detainee strategy. Amb Crocker leaving after very successful tenure.

In other words, Congressman Hoekstra tweeted when he landed in Iraq on a previously secret trip.

The Response and Consequences: Hoekstra stopped tweeting a few days into the trip. He said that he had done nothing wrong and that he was simply doing the same thing that other elected officials had done: discussing when they made trips to foreign areas. However, no one had ever live-tweeted a previously embargoed trip. Hoekstra also said that the Twitter updates he made may not have been accurate. Of course, this is not a message that any elected official wants to send: I may use Twitter to discuss a previously embargoed trip, but don't worry, I don't use it accurately.

Media organizations knew about the trip; however, out of respect to security concerns, they were not going to report on it until all participants returned home. Of course, the trip became fair game once Hoekstra began tweeting about it. The Pentagon said that they would review their security policies for future visits, saying that they would have to be updated to be more in-line with social networking technology.

This was 2009, so Twitter was still an emerging media that had not garnered the attention or user base that it has today. That year was an explosive year for Twitter, as its membership grew 1,382 percent. By the time 2009 was done, the network had over 58 million members. The Hoekstra story helped to illuminate the incredible potential – both good and bad – of Twitter.

Congressman Hoekstra would leave Congress to run for governor in 2010, but lost to eventual Governor Rick Snyder. In 2012, he challenged Senator Debbie Stabenow but would lose that race 59 percent to 38 percent.

The Lesson:

- Respect secrecy and confidentiality: Laws, policies and non-disclosure agreements can all easily be broken via Twitter. Secrecy and confidentiality are absolutely paramount for any public official using social media. Make sure that you aren't running afoul of these concerns when tweeting.

- Check your policy: Given the Pentagon's policy of not revealing a congressional delegation's arrival until they actually arrived, Hoesktra was in line with security concerns. However, it's doubtful that his arrival tweet, or subsequent ones that highlighted the trip's itinerary, were sound from a safety and security perspective. Elected officials should not only strive to make sure they are not violating any laws or any security concerns, but should make sure they are following the spirit any relevant laws and policies. As a rule of thumb: If you aren't sure, don't tweet.

Chapter Twelve:

The most awkward speech of all time

The Background: Phil Davison was a councilman in Minerva, Ohio. In September of 2010, he applied to become the Republican Party's nominee for treasurer in Stark County, Ohio, after the previous candidate was forced out following an embezzling scandal. Any candidate who sought the nomination had to make a presentation to the Stark County Republican Committee.

The Fail: Davidson's six-minute presentation has become the stuff of YouTube legends. Davison's delivery was stilted, awkward and halting. He screamed portions of his speech and often seemed close to crying. The entire speech was filled with uncomfortable pauses, inappropriate emphasis and mistakes in both pacing (speed of the speech) and pacing (he was literally pacing during the speech). Notable quotes included:

- "[I have a] Master's Degree in Communication!!!" Delivered while shouting and without the slightest hint of irony.

- "I will not apologize for my tone tonight. I have been a Republican in times good and I have been a Republican in times bad!"

- "Albert Einstein issued one of my most favorite quotes in the history of the spoken word and it is as follows: 'In the middle of opportunity'...excuse me... 'In the middle of difficulty lies opportunity!' I'm gonna repeat that so I have clarity tonight..."

- "I'm coming, both barrels, guns loaded!"

- "Drastic times require what? [waits for crowd response] DRASTIC MEASURES, YES! Who said that? Thank you!!"

The Response and Consequences: Before the original video was taken down, it was watched more than 2.3 million times. It went viral, earning TV appearances on international news outlets including Politico, CBS, NBC, CNN, Fox News, ABC, the Huffington Post, and *The Daily Mail*. To his credit, Davidson embraced his fame, giving multiple interviews and appearing on comedy shows like *Tosh.0*. He said he was surprised by the reaction to his speech but also surprised that he got no feedback, positive or negative, the day he delivered it.

Sadly for fans of awkward speeches everywhere, Davison lost the nomination to Alexander Zumbar, the finance director of nearby North Canton, Ohio.

The Lesson:

- Cameras are everywhere: Running for office means that everything you say or do can be made fit for the public record, like it or not. As a result, you always have to behave as if the cameras are rolling. Given how popular cameras on phones are, this could very well be the case.

Chapter Thirteen:

Buying social media support – Part One

The Background: Newt Gingrich was once one of the most powerful men in America. From 1995-1998, he served as Speaker of the United States House of Representatives where he was the architect of the 1994 Republican Revolution that saw Republicans take control of the House and Senate for the first time in decades. After pursuing an impeachment of the president and suffering through surprising losses for the Republican Party in 1998, Gingrich faced a coup from within his caucus and resigned from the House. He remained active in the think-tank, non-profit and business world, and in 2012, launched a run for president.

One of Gingrich's strengths was his active social media presence. In August 2011, Gingrich had over 1.3 million Twitter followers – or as he liked to brag, more than six times as many followers as every other Republican presidential candidate combined.

The Fail: In August 2011, a former Gingrich staffer told Gawker that 90 percent of Gingrich's followers were completely fake. The staffer said, "Newt employs a variety of agencies whose sole purpose is to procure Twitter followers. About 80 percent of those accounts are inactive or are dummy accounts created by various 'follow agencies,' another 10 percent are real people who are part of a network of folks who follow others back and are paying for followers themselves (Newt's profile just happens to be a part of these networks because he uses them, although he doesn't follow back), and the remaining 10 percent may, in fact, be real, sentient people who happen to like Newt Gingrich."

The next day, Gawker ran a follow-up story with this headline: "Update: Only 92% of Newt Gingrich's Twitter Followers Are Fake." The story noted that a networking search firm, PeekYou, had looked at Gingrich's followers and determined that barely more than 100,000 were real people. The firm did note that the average Twitter follower had 35-60 percent fake followers, but Gingrich's numbers were obviously higher than that.

The Response and Consequences: The day after the Gawker story broke, Gingrich's campaign spokesman, R.C. Hammond (@rchammond) responded via Twitter:

> @Gawker Gaffes. Hoodwinks readers. Insults 1.3 million .@newtgingrich.@twitter followers. Report is #rude #unfounded & #erroneous.

In a statement later that same day, Hammond told ABC news that, "We've never utilized firms, agencies, or outside organizations to inflate Newt's Twitter followers." Gingrich's campaign also noted that Gingrich was on Twitter's suggested users list; this allowed Gingrich's Twitter account to be promoted in a special section of Twitter's website. Numerous other politicians appeared on the list, though most did not have as high a following as Gingrich.

The timing could have been worse for Gingrich's campaign, but not by much. In June 2011, Gingrich had experienced staff resignations en masse, as his staffers were upset with the direction of his campaign and a perceived lack of commitment from Gingrich. At the time of the scandal, Gingrich was at a mere 7 percent in the most recent national poll, putting him in 5th place. The Twitter story was another in a series of bad press for Gingrich that would add to his difficult summer.

The Lesson:

- Be genuine: Social media is supposed to be all about transparency and honesty; these values are, of course, not reflected in the purchase of Twitter followers. Besides, artificially inflating your follower account defeats the purpose of social media. The size of your network is irrelevant if it isn't real and you aren't influencing real people. Gingrich was trying to show the world how effective he was in this arena and score good news coverage,

55

but the risk (being exposed) far outweighs the rewards (a quick news hit about how you have a lot of Twitter followers).

- If you aren't genuine, don't brag: The day before the Gawker story broke, Gingrich was quoted in the *Marietta Daily Journal* bragging about his high Twitter following: "It turns out I have six times as many Twitter followers as all the other candidates combined," boomed Gingrich. This is the equivalent of a person who robbed a bank bragging about their newfound wealth; it is a statement that invites trouble. If you are doing something less than genuine, don't brag about the positive results.

- Don't buy followers - use ads instead: Facebook, Twitter, YouTube and just about every major social network offer paid ads that will promote your account. This is an accepted practice and a great way to boost your numbers without resorting to any "black flag" techniques. If you want to quickly boost your social media following, this is the way to go.

Chapter Fourteen:

Buying social media support – Part Two

The Background: Like many branches of the United States Government, the State Department has an active presence on social media. In July 2013, the State Department's official Facebook page had more than 280,000 likes, with thousands more spread out on over 150 subsidiary accounts.

The Fail: As first reported by the website DiploPundit, the U.S. Office of Inspector General (OIG) conducted a report on the State Department's Bureau of International Information Programs (BIIP). The goal of the BIIP is to "support the places, content, and infrastructure needed for sustained conversations with foreign audiences to build America's reputation abroad."

Many items came to light in the report, including:

- Two campaigns, initiated in 2011 and 2012, sought to increase the number of likes on "four thematic Facebook properties" through advertising. In total, $630,000 was spent on the campaigns, which increased Facebook likes by over 1,900,000.

- A mere 2 percent of all likes were actually engaging with the page in the form of liking posts, making comments or shares. This, combined with changes to Facebook that made pages disappear from the News Feed if an individual didn't engage with the page, made the OIG question the effectiveness of the campaign.

- The lack of engagement caused the advertising spend of the State Department to shift from gaining likes to increasing engagement through the purchasing of Sponsored Stories, which increased the chances of a story appearing in an individual's News Feed.

- However, the advertising was not tied to any social media strategy. The reason? There was no strategy. Additionally, the State Department controlled over 150 Facebook accounts, but the accounts were all uncoordinated and often posted overlapping or duplicative content.

The Response and Consequences: Coming less than a year after the attacks in Benghazi and in the hyper-partisan environment that followed President Obama's reelection, conservative media outlets were quick to jump on what they perceived to be a waste of taxpayer dollars. "Remember all this when Democrats saddle up to defend their irresponsible spending by insisting that not an ounce of fat can be trimmed from this ridiculously bloated government, so spending cuts mean cops and teachers hitting the unemployment lines?" asked Human Events, a conservative website. "Do you know how many White House Tours they could have had with that?" quipped Clayton Morris, guest host on *Fox & Friends*, in reference to the ongoing sequester which temporarily stopped tours of the Executive Mansion.

The State Department was quick to say that they would implement the recommendations in the OIG's report by October 2013. They also immediately reduced the amount they paid on advertising to $2,500 a month.

In the end, no one was fired and no one lost their jobs. As of 2014, the State Department said they were in the process of implementing the common sense recommendations of creating an overall social media strategy and aligning their advertising with that strategy.

The Lesson:

- Using taxpayer dollars means you are held to a higher standard: If a private company with the reach, power and revenue that the State Department has engaged in a social media advertising campaign to the tune of $630,000, no one would bat an eye. However, taxpayer-funded advertising campaigns are appropriately held to a higher standard. This is particularly true during a time of austerity, when the federal government has cut discretionary spending. In fiscal times like this, justifying a $630,000 advertising campaign is difficult to say the least.

- Align advertising with your overall plan: From a strategic perspective, the most damaging item in the OIG report is that the advertising buys were being made with no overall strategy. Who was the State Department targeting? Were they looking to increase their overall reach or engagement? What were their overall goals and objectives, and how did this connect to the overall mission of the State Department? These are important questions to answer before engaging in any social media campaign, but particularly one that used taxpayer dollars.

Chapter Fifteen:

Don't use Twitter to insult your boss, brag about drinking

The Background: Congressman Rick Larsen, first elected in 2001, is a Democrat who serves Washington's 2nd District. Like all congressmen, he has a complement of staffers that deal with constituents' requests. In December 2011, three of those staffers were Legislative Assistants Seth Burroughs, Elizabeth Robbee and Legislative Correspondent Ben Byers.

The Fail: In a series of tweets that went on for months but accelerated during the "December to Remember" of 2011, the trio committed a variety of fireable offenses, then bragged about them on Twitter. Among the unethical, immoral and potentially illegal behavior they tweeted about:

- Starting a workday with a round of shots on the steps of the Cannon House Office Building.

- Watching YouTube videos during the workday and bragging about it. From Seth Burroughs: "Dear taxpayers — I hope you don't mind that I'm watching YouTube clips of Nirvana at my government job. Thanks, you're the best."

- Insulting their boss, with Burroughs tweeting that Congressman Larsen was an "idiot" and "selfish asshole" and noting that Robbee had called him a "pussy."

- Being too drunk, at work, to pass a field sobriety test, caused in no small part by the shots of Jack Daniels that they were sneaking into their coffee.

The Response and Consequences: Congressman Larsen deserves credit for a very quick response. The story first appeared in the Daily Marker, a conservative blog that covers politics in Washington State and Oregon. Twelve hours later, this story appeared on *The Hill*: "Three congressional staffers canned after tweets reveal in-office partying." Larsen spokesman Bryan Thomas made the following statement: "We became aware of the issue through a tweet referencing an article about the incident. Congressman Larsen immediately decided to fire the three staff members involved in the incident. Congressman Larsen is disappointed by their actions and takes this very seriously. He has made it clear that he will not tolerate this kind of behavior. "

The Lesson:

- Don't put it in writing: It seems amazing that this even needs to be said. Everyone has, at one point or another, insulted their boss and engaged in behavior that they would rather not be broadcasted to the universe. That being said, do not brag about unethical and illegal behavior on Twitter. More to the point, don't just avoid bragging on Twitter; don't put it in an Email, a text, a carrier pigeon or any other form of writing. This can, very easily, come back to haunt you.

Chapter Sixteen:

Holy balls!

The Background: From 2002-2006, Phill Kline served as the attorney general of Kansas. In 2006, he was defeated by Johnson County District Attorney Paul Morrison. Kline, who was a resident of Johnson County, was appointed to fill the remainder of Morrison's term as county district attorney. However, in 2008, he was defeated in the Republican primary by Steve Howe. In 2011, Kline was found guilty of a number of ethics violations, based on his pursuit of abortion clinics, and the Kansas State Board of Discipline of Attorneys recommended that Kline's license be indefinitely suspended. Kline appealed that ruling to the Kansas Supreme Court.

At the same time, Sarah Peterson Herr (@sparklylillife) worked as a research attorney in the Kansas Court of Appeals. Herr worked in the same building as the Kansas Supreme Court.

The Fail: To say thatHerr extremely disliked Kline would be a serious understatement. On November 15, 2012, she watched Kline's appeal of his disciplinary hearing live on her office computer. During that time, she sent out the following tweets:

Holy balls. There are literally 15 cops here for the Phil Kline case today. Thus, I actually wore my badge.

You can watch that naughty, naughty boy, Mr. Kilein, live! live.kscourts.org/live.php

You don't think a sealed document is meant to be confidential BURN

This is a fuzzy situation. Umm, no, sorry Phil.

ARE YOU FREAKIN KIDDING ME. WHERE ARE THE VICTIMS? ALL THE PEOPLE WITH THE RECORDS WHO WERE STOLEN.

Why is Phil Klein smiling? There is nothing to smile about, douchebag.

I love that Phil is all talking about Dr. Tiller like they are cool, and not that his witch hunt helped lead to Dr. Tiller's murder.

"I appreciate the question...but I refuse to answer it. So, here's a picture of a pony."- Phil Klein

Q – How do you get to re-categorize the grand jury's request? A – They liked my pony?

"There are four things." I can't find them. "I mean, there are three things." I see only two. "There are two things."

I might be a little too feisty today...

It's over...sorry. I did like how the district court judges didn't speak the entire time. Thanks for kicking to the SC Phil! Good call!

@awright922 The dc judges sat silently and the 4 appellate judges teamed him. The opinion won't be out for a while.

@awright922 I predict that he will be disbarred for a period not less than 7 years.

The Response and Consequences: On November 16, 2012, the day after the tweets were first sent, Herr was suspended from her position. For the next 15-45 minutes, she had access to her office computer. During that time, she deleted the errand tweets and later admitted that there was "a possibility" that she had deleted her internet browser history. That day, Herr issued a statement in which she apologized for her actions. She claimed that she didn't think that her comments would be seen by the public though she recognized that here tweets were, "not appropriate for someone who works for the court system."

On November 21, a formal complaint was submitted by Lawton Nuss, Chief Justice of the Kansas Supreme Court. That same day, Herr emailed the

Judicial Branches Disciplinary Administrator, Stanton Hazlett, about her possible professional misconduct.

On September 3, 2013, a special prosecutor filed a formal complaint against Herr. According to the complaint, Herr may have violated four Rules of Professional Conduct of the Kansas Bar:

- Engaged in conduct involving dishonesty, fraud, deceit or misrepresentation.

- Engaged in conduct that is prejudicial to the administration of justice.

- Stated or implied an ability to influence a government agency or official.

- Engaged in conduct that adversely reflects on the lawyer's fitness to practice law.

Possible punishments for Herr included disbarment; however, in January 2014, a three-judge hearing panel gave Herr an "informal admonishment," the lightest punishment they could have given. Among the reasons for the light sentence was Herr's lack of any previous disciplinary history, her self-reporting of the incident and her cooperation with authorities.

The Lesson:

- Remember who you (might) speak for: One of the pitfalls of working is that, like it or not, your personal views can be very easily conflated for the views of your employer. Herr found this out the hard way. She was clearly giving her personal opinion, but the fact that she was a court officer who actually worked in the same building as Kline's disciplinary hearing opened Herr up to ethics complaints. Herr put herself in a place in which her derogatory and emotional tweets could be confused with those of her employer.

- Self-reporting is good: One interesting thing that jumped out in this scenario is that Herr actually reported herself to the appropriate authorities. Yes, this is like closing the barn door after the damage has been done, as she had already been caught and fired. However, the self-reporting demonstrated that she recognized that she may have done something wrong, which clearly helped her avoid a more serious punishment. From a strategic perspective, as well as a moral one, it's always better to turn yourself in and beg for mercy.

- Don't delete: Herr's honesty in self-reporting was mitigated by her duplicity when she used her office computer to delete her tweets and internet browser history. As the stories in this book have shown time and time again, deleting your tweets is useless. There are instances when it may be appropriate, like when you know that something you have tweeted is wrong and are attempting to acknowledge that wrong by deleting the offending tweet. However, it is essentially impossible to delete a tweet in the hope that no one will notice it. Even deleting a tweet can't remove it from someone's timeline. Herr's ham-handed attempts at cover-up only made her look guiltier.

Chapter Seventeen:

Don't censor the public

The Background: Mike Pence is the Republican governor of Indiana. Prior to his election as governor, Pence served in Congress. While there, Pence developed a reputation as a social conservative who opposed marriage equality. He voted against making discrimination based on sexual orientation illegal and in favor of a constitutional amendment that would define marriage as being between one man and one woman.

The Fail: In late June 2013, the Supreme Court issued a historic decision overturning the federal Defense of Marriage Act. Pence released a statement condemning the decision and restating his support for the federal DOMA and defining marriage as being between one man and one woman. He put the statement on Facebook, and not surprisingly, the comments ignited a firestorm of debate.

The page's "About" section contained a link to Pence's social media policy which, predictably, noted that posts were monitored and would be deleted if they were vulgar or used defamatory language. This is (and should be) standard operating procedure for any government official. That being said, there is a blurry line between what is insulting to the governor personally and what is simply a statement of opinion. In this case, Pence's staff fell on the censorship side of that line and began deleting posts and blocking individuals that were critical but by no means uncivil. Examples included comments such as:

- "I don't understand why grown, educated men are so affraid of gay people having equal rights…"

- "Go right ahead, Mr. Pence. ..You and your ilk are the fringe."

- "Once I am married federally, how can you reasonably say that I am not married in Indiana…"

The Response and Consequences: Initially, the governor stuck to his guns and defended his team, acknowledging the deletions but stating that his communications department was just following their official Facebook policy: "I do know our staff has a long-standing policy that many news organizations have had regarding name-calling and vulgar comments and I'm confident our staff was just administrating that in the way that we do in any other debate."

However, in the face of mounting evidence, Pence was forced to backtrack. Two days after the initial statement, Pence acknowledged that his communications department went too far and apologized via another statement: "On careful review, it appear [sic] that this was not always the case and some comments were being deleted simply because they expressed disagreement with my position. I regret that this occurred and sincerely apologize to all those who were affected." Pence went on to note that his social media policies would be updated and that staff would be better trained on its enforcement. Apparently, this message wasn't received by Pence's staff right away: that same day, more Facebook comments were deleted, despite the fact that they only linked to other websites and contained no vulgarity or insults.

The entire affair was bad for Pence's credibility. As a column on Examiner.com noted, "By breaking the unofficial but golden and number one rule of social media and censoring the public, Pence has lost the most basic and fundamental foundation of a successful social media campaign: trust." The affair also resulted in the creation of an internet campaign against Pence, using www.pencership.com and a #pencership hashtag on Twitter.

Eventually the entire statement was deleted. It is no longer visible on Pence's Facebook page.

The Lesson:

- Get comfortable with criticism: If you are a politician on social media, get used to criticism. Someone simply disagreeing with you is no reason to censor their comments. As this example shows, that can backfire. In the case of more local offices, you can try reasonably responding to criticism to show that you are comfortable having a debate. In the case of a larger office, like Pence's, you can crowd-source your protection. A look at the threads (before they were deleted) shows that many were praising Pence and defending his statement.

- Admit when you are wrong and stick to it: Pence deserves credit for recognizing his error. In a statement, the governor clearly took responsibility for the inappropriate deletions and promised an improved future. That being said, credit Pence earned for the honest mea culpa was quickly lost when additional comments were deleted. This may be as simple as one staffer missing a directive, but it does show a breakdown in Pence's social media management. The broader lesson is to make sure that your social media management team is strong enough to enforce a new policy, particularly one that is more or less created on the fly.

- Have a clear policy and don't be confused over enforcement: As written, Pence's policy was very clear in terms of protecting against negatives, like insults, vulgarity, etc. What it wasn't clear enough about was ensuring that free speech was protected. Indeed, a good political social media policy should have two sections: an "affirmative" section that notes what is protected, and a "negative" section that notes what will be deleted. This will help limit confusion.

Chapter Eighteen:

Not your favorite

The Background: David Cameron (@David_-Cameron) has served as Britain's Prime Minister since May 2010. Cameron started a Twitter account in October 2012, a relatively late time for a high profile politician. Ironically, his late entry was due to fear of making a Twitter gaffe: "Too many tweets might make a twat," Cameron once said.

In September 2013, terrorists from the Islamist group al-Shabaab attacked the Westgate shopping mall in Nairobi, Kenya. The attacks resulted in the deaths of 67, with another 200 injured.

The Fail: In the aftermath of the attack, Cameron issued this fairly standard tweet, offering his condolences and noting that his Foreign Secretary, William Hague, would give a full statement shortly:

I gave my condolences to President Kenyatta after the attack on the #Westgate shopping centre. @WilliamJHague will give a statement soon.

As is natural for a tweet from someone at this level, responses were varied: the tweet was retweeted over 400 times and favorited more than 75. Some responses, however, were not so kind. This tweet came from @AidanBurleyMP:

> @David_Cameron please call off @WilliamJHague. Hasn't Kenya suffered enough today?

The content of the tweet is nearly as bad as the user behind it. The entire account was dedicated to mocking Lord Norman Tebbit. Tebbit was a highly controversial member of former Prime Minister Margaret Thatcher's cabinet. In 1984, a bombing at the Conservative Party conference in Brighton left Tebbit injured and permanently disabled his wife. Tebbit would eventually leave the House of Commons in order to better care for his wife, though he would be given a seat in the House of Lords.

As for the @AidanBurleyMP account. The uncensored version of the username is "Tebbit's Dick," and it features a picture of Tebbit that the parody's bio claimed showed Tebbit in the middle of sex. It actually showed Tebbit in extreme pain, being carried out of the wreckage of the Brighton bombing.

Normally, a tweet like this would go unnoticed, save for the giggles of a few. However, Cameron's account favorited the tweet. For a brief time, it was the only tweet that Cameron had favorited.

The Response and Consequences: The prime minister's office rushed to explain that while Cameron did send out tweets, other members of his staff and the Conservative Party had access to his account and would send out tweets on his behalf and the tweet in question had been favorited by a junior aide. In a statement, a spokesman for Cameron said, "This is a deeply offensive account that the prime minister would never want to be associated with. Clearly, the tweet was favourited by mistake and was removed as soon as it was realised."

The Lesson:

- The smallest things matter: Most people don't notice what tweets another person favorites. However, when you hit a certain level of visibility, or if your favorite tweets that are controversial enough, they can have a huge impact. Indeed, this isn't the first case of a highly visible politician getting in trouble for a tweet they favorited: Sarah Palin was once on the receiving end of negative publicity that came as a result of an Ann Coulter tweet that she favorited. The tweet itself featured a picture of a church sign that referred to "The blood of Jesus against Obama" and our "Taliban Muslim illegally elected President USA: Hussein."

Chapter Nineteen:

Comparing a U.S. Senator to a murderous dictator

The Background: One of 2014's closest watched Senate elections was Senator Mary Landrieu's (D-LA) reelection effort. Landrieu is a Democrat in a red state who voted for Obamacare, thus making her a high profile target for Republicans. In April 2013, Republicans picked up a top-tier challenger to Landrieu when Congressman Bill Cassidy (R-LA) announced that he would run for the seat.

In November 2013, Senate Democrats used the so-called "nuclear option" against Republicans. Tired of what they viewed as unprecedented filibusters against President Obama's judicial nominees, Democrats voted to change Senate rules, enabling them to advance the nomination of judicial appointments with a majority of fifty votes, instead of the super-majority of sixty. All but three Senate Democrats voted for the move, while every Republican voted against it. Landrieu was one of the Democrats who voted yes.

The Fail: This tweet, courtesy of Joel DiGrado (@jmdigrad), who manages Cassidy's campaign:

> Mary Voted To Kill The Filibuster Today... thehayride. com/2013/mary-v... via @sharethis

The tweet took users to a blog called *The Hayride*, which compared Landrieu to Italian dictator Benito Mussolini for her vote. It also featured a photoshopped picture of Landrieu's face on Mussolini's body.

The Response and Consequences: Landrieu's campaign jumped on the tweet. In a statement, Landrieu's campaign manager Adam Sullivan demanded an apology: "Louisiana politics is colorful and spicy, but this picture is downright despicable and disrespectful. Simply tweeting the image was bad enough, but refusing to take it down now is even worse. The Cassidy campaign owes an apology to Sen. Landrieu and should immediately take down this hurtful reminder of one of the worst and most horrific events in world history."

Making matters worse was that DiGrado ignored several calls for comment, which was noted in every story about the incident. Four days after the initial story broke, Congressman Cassidy was asked for comment about the tweet and deflected the question to attack Landrieu for her filibuster-ending vote: "You know, someone told me about that, but what is important about that is the article in which Senator Landrieu voted to give... dictatorial powers to the Democratic Party in the U.S. Senate, and in that now, after 200 and something years of our republic, Democrats in the Senate have the ability to appoint judges... without having any sort of buy-in from Republicans."

The Lesson:

- Some comparisons you just don't make or endorse: It's safe to say that there are some lines that shouldn't be crossed; comparing a United States senator to one of history's worst fascists who was violently executed by his own people is one of those lines. Clearly, DiGrado didn't make such a comparison, but with his tweet, he appeared to endorse it.

- Staff speaks for the candidate: This is another lesson in a very simple political truth: what a staffer says reflects on the candidate. DiGrado should never have sent out a link to such a charged blog entry unless he knew what he was doing and the tweet was quietly sanctioned by the Cassidy campaign. In general, campaign staff should be neither seen nor heard unless intentionally speaking on behalf of the candidate. DiGrado violated this basic rule.

- Pick a direction and go: By not responding to multiple requests for comment, DiGrado lost an opportunity to put his stamp on the message. When contacted by the press, he should have done one of two things: apologize and deleted the tweet, or doubled down by commenting on Landrieu's vote. Instead, DiGrado ducked any comment at all; as such, he lost an opportunity to influence the story.

Chapter Twenty:

What's worse than Nazis, Soviets and Terrorists combined? Obamacare, apparently.

The Background: In December 2013, Bob Rucho (@Senator-BobRucho) was a North Carolina State Senator (R-39) who was serving his seventh term. Rucho is no stranger to using Twitter to express his controversial views. In the past, he used his Twitter account to attack "liberal weenies" and accuse the United States Department of Justice of extortion. On the 50th anniversary of former President Kennedy's assassination, Rucho tweeted that former President Kennedy could have been a "founder and leader of the Tea Party."

The Fail: On December 15, 2013, Rucho made this tweet:

Justice Robert's pen & Obamacare has done more damage to the USA then the swords of the Nazis, Soviets & terrorists combined.

The Response and Consequences: After the initial tweet, Rucho followed up with this:

Those that tweeted, put your thinking caps back on:"The PEN is mightier than the SWORD." Edward Bulwar-Lytton,1839. But surely you knew that.

Rucho isn't the first public official to make an outlandish comparison when it comes to Obamacare. Former Senator Rick Santorum (R-PA) compared it to the apartheid, former Congressman Allen West (R-FL) compared it to a World War II battle, and conservative Dr. Ben Carson compared it to slavery. However, Rucho's tweet did go viral, earning hundreds of retweets and even more negative comments.

Even the N.C. Republican Party said that Rucho's tweet was too much, with Chairman Claude Pope calling the tweet "highly offensive" and saying that Rucho should apologize. The North Carolina Democratic Party went one step further, calling for Rucho's resignation. Unsurprisingly, Democratic spokesman Micah Beasley tied state Republicans to the comments, saying that Rucho was not a "fringe ideologue" but "a fixture of Republican leadership in the North Carolina Senate.

North Carolina Democrats were joined by many other organizations, op-eds, and, perhaps most effectively, Dr. Susan Cernyak-Spatz. Dr. Cernyak-

Spatz is a member of the North Carolina Jewish community and Holocaust survivor who lived through three different concentration camps over a three-year period. Said Dr. Cernyak-Spatz, "I don't know what the man was thinking… I was absolutely flabbergasted in the 20th Century, and I consider North Carolina my home and a civilized state, that anybody would make a remark like that. That was unbelievable."

So, did Rucho apologize? No. In an interview, Rucho stated, "There's no purpose in resigning if you spoke the truth. I believe without any reservation that it's true. I'm not going to back away from it, because I got every right to say what I want to say too. If people took it out of context and wrong, nothing I can do about that."

Ultimately, the voters looked past Senator Rucho's comments. In the May 2014 primary, Senator Rucho defeated his Republican opponent, Matt Arnold, 55-45 percent. Rucho was unopposed in the general election.

The Lesson:

- Apologize: Prior to this tweet, Rucho had a high profile dispute with other Republicans over efforts to reform North Carolina's tax code. When his plan was rebuffed, he attempted to resign as chair of the Senate Finance Committee (the resignation wasn't accepted) and attacked fellow Republicans, including the Speaker of the North Carolina House and the governor, for not adopting his plan. These actions, combined with his outlandish tweets, will do Rucho no favors when it comes to relationship building. It is highly probable that Rucho severely damaged his relationships in the state capitol, and this will make it much more difficult for him to move his agenda.

- Don't go too far: Rucho isn't the first to inappropriately appropriate the use of the term "Nazi" and it isn't something only consigned to the far right; a quick Google Image search of "George Bush Nazi" will reveal no shortage of the same kind of insanity from the extreme left. That being said, even in today's hyperbolic, sound-bite-filled political world, there is such a thing as going too far.

Chapter Twenty-one:

Arizona is a desert racist wasteland

The Background: Joe Fitzgibbon (@joefitzgibbon) is a Washington State Representative (D-34) who was first elected in 2010. Fitzgibbon is the chair of Washington's House Environmental Committee and serves as a Deputy Majority Whip. Like many in Washington State, he is also a passionate Seahawks fan.

The Fail: On December 21, 2013, the Arizona Cardinals upset the Seattle Seahawks with a last minute touchdown, winning 17-10 and keeping their playoff hopes alive. At the same time, the win broke the Seahawks' fourteen-game home winning streak. Seattle fans, naturally, were upset. Some, however, were more upset than others. After the game, Fitzgibbons tweeted:

> Losing a football game sucks. Losing to a desert racist wasteland sucks a lot.

The Response and Consequences: Fitzgibbon quickly deleted the tweet, but it had already been captured and retweeted by many, including reporters. As such, he issued a second tweet that tried to clarify what he meant:

> Upset re hawks loss, and failure of smart immigration reform—shouldn't have conflated the 2 though. Happy holidays, better for both in '14

The second tweet did little to calm the controversy and Fitzgibbon found himself on the receiving end of numerous attacks, including attacks from Washington State Republicans. "To call a multi-racial community like Arizona is racist and a wasteland is the height of intolerance, and disgusting, his holier than thou attitude is an embarrassment," said Keith Schipper, Communications Director for the Washington Republican Party. Even Fitzgibbon's House colleges took to Twitter to attack his remarks, like Republican Representative J.T. Wilcox (@ jtwilcox111):

> Makes us all look bad. RT "MikeBakerAP: here's a screengrab of lawmaker calling AZ a "racist wasteland" after loss: pic.twitter.com/c3nkmojWIB"

In a follow-up interview, Fitzgibbon said he was upset about the game but also angry at Arizona for what he felt was their discriminatory treatment against immigrants, specifically mentioning the state's highly controversial Senate Bill 1070. Among other things, SB1070 allowed for law enforcement to demand the immigration paperwork of anyone suspected of being an illegal immigrant whenever they felt "reasonable suspicion" existed that the individual in question was an illegal immigrant. At first, Fitzgibbon gave a half-hearted apology for the remarks, saying, "If folks are going to take that too seriously, then I'm sorry about that."

Days later, common sense caught up with him and Fitzgibbon issued a real apology in a subsequent interview: "Sometime I mix sports and politics too much in my own brain, and I made a point not very delicately. That was not a kind thing to say, and I'm sorry for what I said. It wasn't fair to most people in Arizona. There are a couple of mistakes. I shouldn't have mixed the two, shouldn't have painted a broad brush, and Twitter is not always the best way to make points like that. That's the lesson I've learned." In a Facebook note, Fitzgibbon expanded upon his apology, acknowledging that he had said something "hurtful" while expressing his regret.

The Lesson:

- Don't confuse the issue: Fitzgibbons had a policy gripe with Arizona over their treatment of immigrants. He also had an issue with the fact that his home football team lost to Arizona's team. For some bizarre reason, he confused the two. Instead of putting up a funny, down-home Twitter update, Fitzgibbons made a bizarre statement that tied football to immigration. In the process, he put himself and the issue he cared about in an extremely negative light. If you want to give your stance on an issue, fine, but don't tie it to something as comparably petty as a sports game.

- Apologize once, and make it good: Fitzgibbon had to apologize twice and it was only the second apology in which he appeared to truly take responsibility and show remorse. The first apology looked immature, while the second looked genuine. If you ever find yourself in a situation where an apology is necessary, do it once, and make it count.

SECTION II

Wrong account

Tweets that were meant for elsewhere

Smart phones have a bad tendency of making us act not so smart. The same people who manage social media accounts for VIPs are usually active social media users themselves. Sometimes, they confuse their accounts with the accounts of their bosses. As a result, hilarious messages not meant for public consumption are sent into the world. Even worse, these messages are frequently private, vulgar and sent under the name of a high visibility elected official.

One note on the format of this section, since it differs slightly from the others in this book. Generally speaking, the same lessons can be learned from all of this section's stories. As a result, the lessons have been condensed and can be found at the end of the section.

೫ ೫

Chapter Twenty-two:

U love torturing me w this shit

The Background: Senator Chris Dodd (D-CT) served in the Senate for thirty years, from 1981-2011. In 2008, Dodd ran a disappointing presidential campaign and dropped out after finishing seventh place in the Iowa caucuses. After a scandal broke in which Dodd was accused of receiving preferential rates for a mortgage refinancing, Dodd announced his retirement in 2010.

The Fail: On November 18, 2010, barely two weeks after the 2010 elections, Dodd's official Twitter account sent out this errant tweet to Dodd's 13,000+ followers:

U love torturing me w this shit

The Response and Consequences: The tweet was deleted but not before being retweeted, favorited and captured via screenshot. Dodd's office then sent out this tweet:

From Dodd Staff – Apologies to Dodd's followers, last tweet was not from Chris Dodd.

That was followed by this statement: "Due to a technical mistake, a message was inadvertently sent from Senator Dodd's twitter account. Senator Dodd did not send the message. We have corrected the situation and apologize to his followers for the mistake and inappropriate language used in the message."

The parodies of this tweet were brutal. "Do I hear the sound of an intern getting fired?" asked @evanhughes, an author. "Was this meant for Angelo Mozilo?" questioned @Michellemalkin, conservative commenter, referring to the CEO of Countrywide Financial, whose firm had been accused of giving the Dodd family preferential rates for mortgage refinancing. The tweet even resulted in the creation of a parody account, @ShitMyDoddSays.

Ultimately, the tweet was irrelevant to Dodd's future career: his term in office was almost up and he was hired as the Chairman and CEO of the Motion Picture Association of America.

Chapter Twenty-three:

The Secret Service does not like Fox News

The Background: The Secret Service is the federal agency that is charged with, among other things, protecting the president, his family and other VIPs. On May 9, 2011, the Secret Service created a Twitter account.

The Fail: A mere nine days after the Secret Service created their Twitter account, @SecretService, the Secret Service sent out this message to over 18,000 followers:

> Had to monitor Fox for a story. Can't. Deal. With. The. Blathering

The Response and Consequences: The tweet was taken down very quickly. In a statement, Special Agent in Charge Edwin Donovan said, "The tweet did not reflect the views of the U.S. Secret Service and it was immediately removed. We apologize for this mistake… policies and practices which would have prevented this were not followed and will be reinforced for all account users. We will ensure existing policies are strictly adhered to in order to prevent this mistake from being repeated, and we are conducting appropriate internal follow-up." Donovan was also placed in the awkward position of having to explain why Secret Service agents were watching Fox News ("Our public affairs employees monitor all the news channels throughout the day for stories that effect the Secret Service") and what story the employee was watching when that tweet was sent out ("I don't know"). Incidentally, Fox News had run a story that day about a 13 year old who was interviewed by the Secret Service after posting on Facebook that the president should watch out for terrorists' attacks after killing Osama Bin Laden.

According to Donovan, the person who had sent the tweet "no longer has access to our official account," meaning that this one saw someone's job responsibilities curtailed, if it didn't result in an outright firing.

Chapter Twenty-four:

The fourteen second tweet

The Background: The Super Bowl is known for its blockbuster commercials that are frequently racy and controversial. In February 2013, one of those ads featured the two actresses from the CBS show *Two Broke Girls* in skimpy clothing, dancing on a stripper pole. The ad, however, was a parody: it also featured nerdy men ogling and the girls realizing that they are only dancing sexy for the Super Bowl.

Meanwhile, Idaho's sole congressman was Raul Labrador (@Raul_Labrador), who had been in office since 2010.

The Fail: This tweet, sent by the congressman:

Me likey Broke Girls.

The Response and Consequences: Labrador's office apologized for the errand tweet. Labrador is a Mormon and a conservative, so this certainly didn't line-up with his image. In calls after the incident,

Hardy acknowledged that he had sent the tweet but called it "totally an accident."

Hardy was fired for the tweet. Fourteen seconds is apparently all it takes to ruin a career.

Chapter Twenty-five:

Don't confuse texting and twitter

The Background: In 2009, challengers were lining up to take out U.S. Senator Bob Bennett (R-UT), the three-term senator. Conservatives argued that Bennett was not conservative enough and were angered over his support for the Bush bank bailouts and what they felt was insufficient conservative principles. Utah's party nomination process is different than most states, as its nominees can be determined at a party convention, rather than a primary election. If a candidate receives more than 60 percent of the vote at the convention, they become the party nominee; if not, the top two candidates advance to a primary.

One candidate who had expressed an interest in running was Mark Shurtleff (@markshurtleff), the Utah attorney general. Shurtleff was elected in 2000 and then reelected in 2004 and 2008. In May 2009, Shurtleff was widely believed to be preparing for challenge to Bennett, though he had yet to make his campaign official. Shurtleff was the only state-wide office holder to be considering running against Bennett, so his candidacy was a very serious one.

The Fail: The campaign's secret announcement was ruined when Shurtleff confused texting with Twitter and told the world about his campaign announcement and strategy in a series of tweets. While in Israel on a trade mission, Shurtleff tweeted the following:

> Yeah, pretty weird. I was supporting another candidate for state party chair and polls showed tim losing so maybe he's getting back. Altho

> Ith all of the legislative conservative causcus and other senators and representative there endorsing me. Time to rock and roll! I have ...

> ing, it will also be against Bennett and I'll pick up his delegates when he drops off the first ballot. I'm announcing I'm running at 12

> No, I just realized that I was responding from a text from u. I'm going to pull it off immediately.

The Response and Consequences: Shurtleff admitted his mistake, deleted the tweets and responded with some humor:

> Thinking of "texting while drowsy" law after private 1AM tweet went public. Formal

announcement on 5/20 about senate race and tweeting plans.

The cat now completely out of the bag, Shurtleff went on to announce his candidacy and campaign against Bennett.

The story went national, and though all candidates want this kind of attention, Shurtleff probably didn't want to get his campaign off to this kind of start. Ultimately, the race was not to be for Shurtleff. He withdrew from the race in November 2009, about eight months before the convention. Shurtleff cited the need to spend time with his daughter, who was in a treatment facility, dealing with severe depression.

Incidentally, this would not be Shurtleff's last run-in with Twitter. Shurtleff would later make national news for live-tweeting the final legal mechanisms involved in the execution of Ronnie Lee Gardner, who had been convicted of murder.

Chapter Twenty-six:

The lesson from tweets that were sent from the wrong account

As has become painfully apparent, tweets meant for one account frequently wind up elsewhere. That being said, they all share roughly the same common thread and thus present the same learning opportunity. Here are the lessons from these tweets:

- Careful from what account you are tweeting: This is a lesson that comes up frequently in this chapter. Make sure you know what account you are tweeting from. Programs like Hootsuite can make this mistake way, way, too easy. If you are saying something sensitive or personal, take a moment before tweeting to make sure that you are, in fact, using the right account.

- Use different management accounts: A relatively simple way to lessen the odds of making this mistake is to use different management accounts for different accounts. Use Hootsuite for work and TweetDeck for your personal account. Linking your personal and professional accounts makes it easier to make this mistake while keeping them separate helps to decrease the odds.

- Set up a policy for an accidental tweet: Always be prepared, because all of the caution in the world may not stop a rogue tweet. As such, if you are a staffer, have an official policy in place about what to do in the event of an accidental tweet. A good policy, roughly, can be summed up as follows:

    (a) Delete the tweet.

    (b) Tell your superiors.

    (c) Release a statement saying that a tweet was sent out, by a staffer, from the wrong account. Emphasize that the tweet did not come from the elected official (as Senator Dodd did after his errand tweet) and that steps are being taken to ensure that the mistake doesn't happen again in the future.

    (d) Apologize profusely to your boss and beg for mercy.

- Don't claim you were hacked: Many individuals, including Congressman Anthony Weiner, have said they were hacked when a tweet went public that wasn't supposed to. Stop it. Don't do that. You just look stupid. Eventually, the truth always comes out. Be honest. Say a tweet went out on the wrong account and that new policies are being put into place to make sure it doesn't happen again. When you say you were hacked and you weren't, you lose credibility.

SECTION III

Sex

Keep it in your pants and off the internet

Very few things capture the public's imagination like a sex scandal. Social media gives an added dimension to sex scandals, since video, pictures or texts are usually involved and easy to disseminate. As a result, social media brings sex scandals to a whole new level of "visibility" – and one that most of us would probably be better off without! Here is proof that sex is one of those things that is best left off of the internet, particularly if you are an elected official or candidate.

Chapter Twenty-seven:

The Craigslist Congressman

The Background: Congressman Chris Lee (R-NY) was elected to serve the 26th District of New York State in 2008. Lee was reelected in 2010 with 76 percent of the vote. At the time of his reelection, the 46-year-old Lee was married and had one child.

The Fail: That would be this:

This scandal started on January 14, 2011, less than two weeks after Lee had been sworn in for a second term. As reported by Gawker, a 34-year-old woman posted an ad in the "Women seeking Men" portion of Craigslist. Later that day, Congressman Chris Lee responded from a Gmail account, using his real name. In the Email, he claimed to be a 39-year-old divorced lobbyist (literally nothing about that description is accurate). He also sent the above picture and engaged in a relatively tame, flirtatious conversation.

After Googling Lee, the woman discovered his real identity and stopped talking to him. She then sent the entire conversation to Gawker, who reported the story on February 9, 2011.

The Response and Consequences: When first contacted by Gawker, Lee's spokesman claimed that Lee had been hacked. The spokesman denied that Lee had ever posted on Facebook, except to sell furniture. The spokesman also made sure to confirm that the congressman was happily married.

That explanation didn't last long. Lee announced his resignation three hours after the Gawker story first broke. In a statement, Lee admitted (more or less) what he had done:

"It has been a tremendous honor to serve the people of Western New York. I regret the harm that my actions have caused my family, my staff and my constituents. I deeply and sincerely apologize to them all. I have made profound mistakes and I promise to work as hard as I can to seek their forgiveness.

"The challenges we face in Western New York and across the country are too serious for me to allow this distraction to continue, and so I am announcing that I have resigned my seat in Congress effective immediately."

Adding insult to injury: in a special election held barely three months later, the seat switched from red to blue, as Democrat Kathy Hochul took advantage of a schism in the Republican Party and beat Republican Jane Corwin and Tea Party nominee Jack Davis.

The Lesson:

- Cheating on your spouse? Don't put it in writing: This is career-endingly stupid. In the best of circumstances, cheating on your spouse is bad enough. If you are an elected official and you engage in extra-marital relationships, you shouldn't seek it on Craigslist.

Chapter Twenty-eight:

Do not grope cardboard cutouts of the Secretary of State

The Background: At 27, Jon Favreau had the job of a lifetime. A speechwriting wizard, Favreau was the newly appointed Director of Speechwriting for President-Elect Barack Obama. Favreau had worked with Obama since Obama's election to the United States Senate and had previously worked for the Kerry presidential campaign.

The Fail: In December 2008, Favreau attended a party held by friends. Cameras and alcohol were present (a terrible combination if there ever was one), and at one point, this photo was snapped.

Favreau, on the left, can be seen groping a cardboard cutout of then Secretary of State nominee Hillary Clinton while a friend feeds her a beer bottle. The picture was on Facebook for two hours before Favreau removed it; of course, by then, it was far too late:

The Response and Consequences: Favreau called Senator Clinton to apologize. To Clinton's infinite credit (and to Favreau's infinite luck), the Clinton camp responded with humor. In the aftermath, Clinton spokesman Philippe Raines commented, "Senator Clinton is pleased to learn of Jon's obvious interest in the State Department and is currently reviewing his application."

The pic still generated negative press. Many pundits, like CNN's Campbell Brown, noted that this seemed to be another example of sexism coming from the president-elect's camp, with Brown questioning why Clinton was letting Favreau's grope go: "Put another woman in that photo, just an average woman who supported you during the campaign. Have it be her image being degraded by a colleague of hers. Would you be OK with that?" However, aside from some embarrassing press, the story blew over. Favreau served as Obama's Director of Speechwriting until February 2013, when he stepped down to take a job in the private sector.

The Lesson:

- At a party? Avoid cameras: Given the prevalence of social media and cameras among 20-30 somethings, it is highly probable that many individuals will run into problems if they seek public office (indeed, see later chapters of the book for further examples). However, it is possible to minimize risk. Try not to get photographed doing stupid things. And this goes double for individuals who are already in (or will be seeking) public office. It is difficult to erase past mistakes but it's easier to prevent future ones.

- Conduct a social media audit: Thinking about running for public office one day? Conduct your own social media audit. Go back and look at all your comments, all your photos, all the Facebook groups you joined, etc. See anything that you don't want on the front page of your newspaper?

Delete it. Unsure? Delete it. Better safe than sorry, and if you are running for office, people will be looking.

Chapter Twenty-nine:

Congressional candidate photographed in compromising positions

The Background: In October 2013, Stewart Mills kicked off his campaign for Minnesota's 8th Congressional seat. A Republican, Mills was seeking to challenge Democrat Rick Nolan, who was first elected in 2012. Mills' challenge was a serious one: in the 3rd quarter of 2013, Mills doubled Nolan's fundraising haul, an impressive accomplishment for a challenger and a testament to just how serious of a campaign Mills is set to run.

The Fail: Barely a month after his campaign kick-off, Mills was making headlines, but not in a good way. Embarrassing Facebook photos were found by the *Minnesota City Pages*. The pictures showed Mills drinking from a beer bong and licking the lips of another woman who is not his wife.

The Response and Consequences: Mills released an unapologetic statement following the publication of the pics. "It's no secret that in the past I've let my hair down to have fun with family and friends. My wife and I have had many lighthearted moments in our lives but right now I am focused on my Congressional campaign and the disastrous effects of our overreaching government and sky high unemployment in the north eastern Minnesota."

As the Mediate blog correctly noted, the statement was not an apology. "It was a seemingly straightforward and unapologetic response from a man whose potential constituents could easily be turned off by the photos. Evidently, Mills was banking that Minnesota voters would let his relatively minor discretions slide."

Aside from Mills' statement and embarrassing press, the Mills campaign carried on. Mills ran uncontested for the Republican nomination in the primary on August 12, 2014, but was defeated by incumbent Rick Nolan in the general election on November 4, 2014.

The Lesson:

- Conduct opposition research on yourself: It's pretty clear that this wasn't the first time Mills attended a party like this. Before announcing his campaign, Mills should have paid someone to conduct opposition research on himself and see what negative information was out there. Even a relatively inexperienced opposition researcher could have found these pictures and had them removed.

- If you know what's out there, admit it early: When Mills first started running for Congress, he should have known that pictures like this could surface to haunt his campaign. Mills could have prepared for this by admitting early that he had been a partier in the past but had since matured. After all, countless politicians have won elections after being caught making far more serious transgressions.

- Know what is visible: The beer-bong photo was posted by Mills' wife in 2009; the woman-licking pic was on the Facebook profile of Mills' step-daughter. Mills had to know that these pictures (or ones like them) were available and should have had them taken down. Unfortunately, these days, when a candidate starts to run for office, they have to check what Facebook photos they are tagged in and have embarrassing ones removed. This is a good rule of thumb, even for people who aren't running for Congress. Indeed, the beer bong photo was online until Mills' declared his campaign, while the woman-licking photo was removed only after the first *City Pages* report was published.

- Be careful at parties: The pictures were posted in 2009. Facebook had already taken off and Mills was a prominent member of his family business at the time. He had no business being so careless in an area where digital cameras were snapping. He should have exhibited more caution.

Chapter Thirty:

China's Anthony Weiner

The Background: Xie Zhiqiang was the head of the Liyang City Sanitation Bureau, located in Southern China. In 2011, after attending a class reunion, he was convinced to open a Weibo account (Weibo is a Chinese version of Twitter). It all pretty much went downhill from there.

The Fail: Zhiqiang was having an affair with a local business executive. He used Weibo to communicate with her; the conversations included sexting and setting up future rendezvous. Among the conversations:

Mistress: Dear Pangpang [nickname], I will be at Muhu tomorrow, give me a call.

Xie: How will you give me the hotel room card, I will not take it from reception by myself.

Xie: Get me the hotel room card. Take a break in the hotel and I will be right over, ok?

Xie: Honey, we should not make phone calls or SMS's. This is Meet on Weibo, I miss you so much, let's decide on Weibo where to go, ok?

Okay, so clearly this is not good for Zhiqiang's marriage and definitely not good for his career, but not the end of the world, right? Maybe. That is, until this gem:

Xie: Did you buy anything in Shanghai? I will take care of the reimbursing.

Setting up an extra-marital affair on government time is definitely bad. Offering to use tax dollars to reimburse your mistress is much, much worse.

Zhiqiang thought that he was sending private messages. What he didn't know was that the Internet was laughing at him, as every message he sent was publicly visable. It was so bad that a group of people in China were copying Zhiqiang's conversations to a separate website for their own amusement.

The Response and Consequences: This went on for two weeks before Zhiqiang was confronted by a reporter from China's *Modern Express*. He was stunned that his affair – and crimes – were visible to the world. "How can you see them? They are not visible, right? You saw all the Weibos we sent each other? It can't be."

It was. In an emergency meeting of the Liyang municipal legislature, Zhiqiang was suspended and put under investigation. In a report to his superiors,

Zhiqiang admitted his mistake. "My recent flirtation with a woman on Sina Weibo was exposed to the public. I had no idea until reporters knocked on my door. I still don't understand how other people could read my personal message to a woman, in fact the whole country... I thought I was very discrete, I had no idea that I ruined my career and hurt my family." He then tried to place the blame elsewhere. "The Chinese Internet is morally bankrupt, everyone is looking to violate someone's privacy on the Internet."

The Lesson:

- Know what you are using: Other chapters have covered the fact that you need to be extraordinarily careful with what you put in writing. Here is a slightly different turn on that principle: make sure you understand what technology you are using and know how to use it. If Zhiqiang had actually understood Weibo, this entire story would never have happened. He didn't realize that his supposed private messages were, in fact, public ones. When you hold a public position, you are far more visible. As such, you need to make sure you know how to use whatever you are using. Read a tutorial. Watch a YouTube video. Just make sure you know what you are doing because any mistake you make will be magnified as a result of your position.

Chapter Thirty-one:

Like a rabbit: The sexting adventures of Tony Phillips

The Background: Tony Phillips was elected as a Democrat to Allentown City Council in 2005. After repeated fights with fellow Democrat, Mayor Ed Pawlowski, Phillips switched to the Republican Party and began a campaign for mayor.

The Fail: In September 2005, a woman who went by the name of Delores released a Facebook chat that she had with Phillips. The chat was exceptionally raunchy. Dolores posted the transcript with this note: "is this the kind o man we want to mayor for Allentown? 1st he had a woman at the park n now he is tryin to pick women uo on facebook. Shame on Tony Phillips." Phillips, who was separated from his wife, already came with baggage. In 2007, Phillips was cited by police for being in a public park, in the middle of the night, with a woman, under playground equipment.

In the conversation, Phillips actually attempted to use some discretion and steer the conversation away from Facebook, telling Delores to "provide another medium of communication if u can." However, Dolores' feminine wiles ultimately captured Phillips' imagination, and they continue to chat. During the conversation, Phillips seems to understand he shouldn't be having this type of conversation, delaying in responding so long to Delores that Dolores asked, "u scared," then "hello." However, Phillips continues to talk to Delores, describing his body type. Delores describes herself as a "freak" and Phillips added, "too much for me." The conversation then manages to get worse, as the two trade some pretty explicit sex talk, culminating with this exchange:

> Delores: ur salad toss
> Phillips: yes like a rabbit
> Phillips: very much so
> Delores: mmmmmmmmmmmmmmmmm
> Phillips: u would have to dig me out of the rabbit hole by my ears
> Phillips: scuba gear required

The Response and Consequences: Phillips publicly considered withdrawing from the race, saying, "I don't know how damning this is, so I will have to wait and see." Ultimately, Phillips remained in the race, though his campaign manager quit.

One week later, Delores came forward: Her real name was Margarita Lopez and she said she had set Phillips up, claiming that she had a four-year relationship with Phillips while he was still married. Lopez said that her relationship with Phillips ended in 2007, after she confronted Phillips about the Bucky

Boyle park incident. During that confrontation, Lopez suffered a fractured elbow and filed a police report, though no charges were ever filed. Phillips admitted to having a relationship with Lopez but then attacked her: "I regretfully was involved with Ms. Lopez three years ago. This was a rough time and wish I had not become involved with this relationship. This was a difficult time in my personal life for both my family and Ms. Lopez. These personal attacks come from someone who has become bitter, upset and have a personal agenda attached to them. She has used deceptive measures to push her personal issue into the public eye. It is unfortunate, that her ongoing issues have manifested themselves in this fashion."

As you'd expect, the affair, cybersex and allegations of beating a woman didn't do wonders for Phillips' campaign. He was crushed, losing 74-26 percent to Mayor Pawlowski.

The Lesson:

- Trust your instincts: During the conversation, Phillips seems to understand that continuing to exchange these raunchy messages is a bad idea... yet he continues it. This is a classic case where a politician's brain was overridden by other emotions. Phillips should have trusted his instincts, and you should trust yours. Does a situation seem like a bad one? Get out of it.

- Don't blame the victim: Once this story broke, there was pretty much nothing that Phillips could have done. The allegations were incredibly damning, particularly the report that Phillips was involved in a physical altercation with Lopez and had fractured her elbow. American politics is replete with examples of cheating spouses who recover (see Bill Clinton). As this election demonstrated, they are much less willing to forgive a man who allegedly had a confrontation with a woman that resulted in injury. Phillip's insensitive statement did not help him. He called Lopez bitter and upset, then said that she had a personal agenda against him. The worst thing any elected official involved in a scandal can do is blame another person. Take responsibility and move on.

Chapter Thirty-two:

Anthony Weiner – Part One

The Background: This is, without a doubt, one of the most well-known social media fails. Democrat Anthony Weiner (@RepWeiner) was elected to Congress in 1998, where he served in New York's 9th District, comprised of southern Brooklyn and southern and central Queens. Weiner was an unapologetic liberal who fervently advocated for progressive causes, including single-payer health care, gun control, gay rights and abortion rights. Weiner was also known to be one of the toughest men in Washington to work for. A *New York Times* article noted that he had one of the highest turnover rates in Congress. According to the article, Weiner had a fiery temper and was known for chewing out his staffers and throwing office furniture. A technology addict, Weiner was one of the biggest users of Twitter in Congress. Before his resignation, Weiner had around 40,000 Twitter followers and used Twitter to personally respond to questions and concerns.

The Fail: The tweet that brought Anthony Weiner down was sent out on May 27, 2011. At the time,

Weiner was talking with Gennette Cordova, a 21-year-old college student in Seattle, when he sent her a tweet that contained a link. The link contained a picture of Weiner's erect penis through his boxers.

The Response and Consequences: The tweet was deleted and Weiner claimed he was hacked, sending out this tweet the next day:

Tivo shot. FB hacked. Is my blender gonna attack me next? #TheToasterIsVeryLoyal

The explanation seemed reasonable, as this had happened before: previous Twitter hacks had temporarily hijacked accounts from countless elected officials, including President Obama. However, things took a turn for the strange on June 1. That day, Weiner went on MSNBC and said that he could not say, "with certitude," if the picture was actually of him. He did, however, fervently deny sending the picture to Cordova. Weiner also hired a private security firm to investigate the tweet and alleged hacking. Weiner would eventually spend $43,100 on that investigation. Later that same day, Weiner suggested that the photo might have been one of him that had been manipulated.

With blood in the water, the media kept investigating the matter. They would hit pay dirt. On June 6, BigGovernment. com published a photo of a man, naked above the waist but with his face out of the picture. The website said that it was a picture of Weiner, provided by a woman with whom Weiner was sexting. The same day, Radar Online published that it had over 200 sexually explicit Facebook messages, allegedly sent by Weiner, to another woman. Among them was Weiner bragging about the "ridiculous bulge in my shorts."

With evidence mounting, Weiner held a press conference in which he made an admission of guilt: "I have made terrible mistakes... I have not been honest with myself, my family, my constituents, my friends and supporters, and the media." At the press conference, Weiner admitted to having sent the original message to Cordova. He also confessed to having engaged in "several inappropriate conversations" with at least six different women and said that the conversations took place both before and during his marriage. At the same press conference, Weiner announced his intention to not resign and remain a congressman. That same day, Minority Leader Nancy Pelosi called for an ethics investigation into Weiner's actions. The reason was "to determine whether any official resources were used or any other violation of House rules occurred." The next day, Reince Preibus (head of the Republican National Committee) and Majority Whip Eric Cantor (R-VA) each called on Weiner to resign.

There was another factor at play. Weiner was not well liked in Congress. In a damning June 2013 article, published by the *New York Times*, Weiner was painted as a narcissistic egomaniac with no ability to play nice with others. Among the allegations:

- Weiner threatened to "torpedo" President Obama's health care package by introducing a broader measure. Weiner backed off only when promised a public role in the debate.

- He passed only one law and it was one pushed by a contributor who had donated five figures to Weiner's campaign.

- Weiner didn't care about Congress and used his seat as a platform to run for mayor of New York (which he tried and failed at in 2005 and 2013).

- Weiner was reckless and didn't care at all about the hard work involved in actually writing laws.

- He only fundraised for the Democratic Party while actively seeking a seat on the coveted Energy and Commerce Committee.

With all this in mind, the Weiner saga continued to get worse. On June 10, four days after Pelosi's call for an ethics investigation, Delaware police announced that they were investigating tweets between Weiner and a 17-year-old New Castle girl. Ultimately, the police concluded that there was nothing inappropriate about the tweets, but it wasn't the headline Weiner needed.

By June 11, half a dozen House Democrats had joined the growing chorus of elected officials calling on Weiner to resign. That same day, Minority Leader Nancy Pelosi (D-CA), Democratic Congressional Campaign Committee head Steve Israel (D-NY) and DNC Chair Debbie Wasserman-Schultz (D-CA) all called on Weiner to resign. Weiner announced that he was requesting a leave of absence to enter a treatment facility in order to focus on "becoming a better husband and a healthier person."

With no support from House leadership and polls showing that a substantial portion of Weiner's constituents wanted him to resign (three separate polls showed that 30 percent, 33 percent and 46 percent of respondents in Weiner's district wanted him to step down), it was only a matter of time. On June 16, Weiner finally gave into the inevitable and announced his resignation. "I had hoped to be able to continue the work that the citizens of my district elected me to do, to fight for the middle class and those struggling to make it. But unfortunately the distraction that I have created has made that impossible."

The Lesson:

- Reputation matters: The most important lesson here is one far broader than social media. Reputation and credibility matter. As previously noted, Weiner simply wasn't liked by his colleagues. He was viewed as too self-serving, arrogant and flashy. Even in Congress, there needs to be limits on this type of behavior. Weiner's scandal was so severe that it probably would have ended his career anyway, but his position would have been greatly solidified if he had actually been liked by his colleagues.

- Own it: The Weiner scandal first erupted with an errant click that Weiner tried to cover up, going so far as to spend tens of thousands in campaign cash to investigate a security breach that he knew had never happened. He first tried to say that there was nothing inappropriate and that he had done nothing wrong, and was very quickly proven to be a liar. Weiner should have owned the mistake as soon as it happened, accepted responsibility and gone into treatment right away. Instead, by trying to engage in a cover-up, Weiner dragged the story out and made it worse. The lesson is this: when caught, admit. Inevitably, the cover-up makes life worse.

- Direct Message vs. a public message – and how there is no difference: The initial picture that included a picture of Weiner's crotch was meant to be sent as a direct message, not a public one. So the lesson here is that politicians should know the difference between a public response and a private one, right? Wrong. The lesson needs to be that there is no difference. Once something has been sent digitally, it can go public. Never, ever, ever put something in writing that you would be uncomfortable being on the front page of your home newspaper. Weiner was done in not only by public messages, but by private ones as well. Once something is in electronic format, it cannot be taken back. That's a lesson that Weiner (among many others) has learned the hard way.

Chapter Thirty-three:

Anthony Weiner – Part Two

The Background: After his ignominious resignation from Congress, Weiner returned to New York City and started a consulting business. However, speculation continued that Weiner would run for mayor and in May 2013, Weiner officially declared his candidacy via YouTube. In the clip, Weiner admitted mistakes but pledged to continue to fight for the middle class. Weiner started the race in great shape: a month after Weiner announced, a poll came out that showed him leading the race with 25 percent, with City Council President Christine Quinn at 20 percent. A May 2013 poll showed that 59 percent of Democrats believed that Weiner deserved a second chance. Indeed, at least at the start of the race, New Yorkers appeared ready to give Anthony Weiner the role he so desperately wanted.

And then the wheels came off. Again.

The Fail: On July 22, *The Dirty* ran a story detailing how Weiner had continued to exchange sexually explicit messages with other women after his resignation from Congress. Of course, this flew in the face of Weiner's promise that he had changed his ways. A series of other allegations, reports and images emerged in addition to the new sexting reports, including:

- Weiner's exposed penis (previous pictures showed his genitals through his boxers only).

- Weiner promised his sexting partner (later identified by Buzzfeed as Sydney Leathers, a 22-year-old activist from Indiana) that he would help her get a job at Politico and a condo in Chicago where they could meet up and have sex.

- Repeated phone sex.

Weiner seemed to know what he was doing was wrong. At one point he asked the girl to "do him a solid" and delete their conversations.

The next day at a press conference (with wife Huma by his side), Weiner admitted to exchanging the messages, which continued for a year after the initial scandal and his resignation from Congress. He claimed that this time, he had stopped for good. Weiner made it clear, however, that he was staying in the race, a decision that was met with disdain from mayoral rivals, women's organizations and even Democratic leader Nancy Pelosi. Pelosi's comments were particularly damning. Referring to Weiner and the then mayor of San Diego, Bob Filner (who had been accused of sexual harassment by multiple women),

Pelosi commented, "If they are clueless, get a clue. If they need therapy, do it in private. The conduct of some of these people that we're talking about here is reprehensible. It is so disrespectful of women, and what's stunning is that they don't even realize."

The Response and Consequences: Weiner's polling numbers entered a free fall. An NBC 4/Wall Street Journal/Marist Poll found that Weiner's favorable/unfavorable ratings among Democrats were at 30/52, a massive drop from the last poll that had Weiner at 52/36. Even worse, Weiner fell from first to second, with Christine Quinn at 25 percent, Weiner at 16 percent and rivals Bill Thompson and Bill de Blasio nipping at his heels with 14 percent. Weiner's poll numbers would only get worse from there.

Weiner pressed on, ignoring calls to drop out of the campaign. Weiner's campaign manager quit five days after the scandal first broke. Mayoral opponent and City Council President Christine Quinn said that Weiner's scandals and total lack of legislative success disqualified him from the race. Congressman Peter King (R-NY), who served with Weiner, said that Weiner was "not psychologically qualified" to be mayor.

As Weiner continued to tank in the polls, his campaign behavior grew more bizarre. In an August interview, Weiner mocked reporters who were following him while he door knocked ("Dude, you gotta get hobby"). He told a British reporter that he felt as if he had "stepped into a Monty Python bit" and saying that it was hard to take her seriously as a result of his accent. Then he yelled at a young staffer in front of reporters for his organizational skills. "This is 'NG,' not great, not great. Oh boy, this is not as well organized as I like."

In the campaign's final days, Weiner changed his focus from yelling at reporters and staffers to voters themselves. When a heckler at a Jewish bakery in Brooklyn called Weiner a scumbag and insulted him for being "married to an Arab" (for the record, Huma Abedin was born in Michigan), Weiner exploded, turning around to argue with the heckler. "You're a perfect person? What Rabbi taught you that you're my judge?" While the man's behavior was obviously repulsive, Weiner forgot that, when running for elected office, the voters are judging you.

Ultimately, the campaign ended the only way it could: catastrophically. First, Weiner lost the election, coming in dead last with almost 5 percent of the vote. Next, Weiner couldn't get into his election night party because Sydney Leathers, the woman who kicked off the newest round of scandals, decided to stand at the party's main entrance. Wearing a low-cut red dress, Leathers said that, "It's my duty to be here." Incidentally, this was after she stood outside of Weiner's headquarters on Election Day, holding a sign that said "Don't vote Weiner: Download Weinerizer" (Weinerizer is the name of Sydney Leathers' music debut). Eventually, Weiner's staff figured out how to get Weiner into the party by having him walk through a neighboring McDonald's that had a shared entrance with the Connolly's Pub and Restaurant, where the party was being held. As Weiner walked through the

McDonald's, reporters literally ran after him, recording the sprint for posterity and uploading videos via Twitter and Vine. Weiner conceded, acknowledging that he was an "imperfect messenger," and thanking his staff, parents and son, but not his wife, who didn't attend the party. To top it off, Weiner flipped off a reporter as he was being driven away. The gesture was captured via photo and video and quickly made the rounds on Twitter.

The Lesson:

- Let it go: This isn't so much a social media lesson as it is a life lesson. Sometimes, you just have to quit. Weiner's run was catastrophic and humiliating. The entire situation is very sad. Instead, he proved that he was incapable of running his own Facebook account, let alone a city of more than eight million people. There comes a point in every life where a person has to make a choice: to continue or give up against incredible odds. Weiner should have given up.

SECTION IV

Hating groups and threatening violence

Racism, sexism, homophobia and violent threats

Few ways of thinking have done more damage to the American spirit and psyche as racism, sexism and homophobia. American political history certainly has no shortage of any of these scourges. At the same time, social media provides cowardly users with an illusion of anonymity under which they can make violent threats. Though it has improved with time, American politics continue to be marred by absurd statements that invoke stereotypes or violence. Social media is replete with this unfortunate content. However, just like in the real world, sunshine is the best disinfectant and social media has helped to expose people, politicians and organizations for their true, repulsive beliefs. Here now are some of the "finest" examples of bigotry and threats, as well as the negative consequences that befell those who expressed these abhorrent viewpoints.

ॐ ८४

Chapter Thirty-four:

The racist version of the Obama Stimulus

The Background: Rutland County is located in western Vermont, along the state's border with New York. With a population of just over 60,000, it is Vermont's second most populated county. The county is overwhelmingly white (more than 90 percent) and has trended increasingly Democratic in the past decade. In 2000, 47.7 percent of the county voted for Al Gore; in 2008, 61 percent voted for Barack Obama.

The Fail: In July 2012, this post appeared on the Rutland, Vermont Republican Party's Facebook page:

> Just wanted to let you know – today I received my 2012 Social Security Stimulus Package. It contained two tomato seeds, cornbread mix, a prayer rug, a machine to blog smoke up my butt, 2 discount coupons to KFC, an "Obama Hope & Change" bumper sticker, and a "Blame it on Bush" poster for the front year. The directions were in Spanish. Watch for yours soon.

It's not easy to simultaneously insult so many different ethnic groups, but this post managed to simultaneously attack African Americans, Muslims and gays. What made the post even worse is that it was made by Rob Towle, Chair of the Rutland GOP.

The Response and Consequences: The post generated several negative comments and was removed from the party's Facebook page, but the damage had already been done. The story was first reported by the local *Green Mountain Daily* on Sunday, July 15. After the posts went up, Towle first tried digging its way out of the post by agreeing with its general spirit:

> Thanks NTodd.....the people that ARE frustrated but the reality contained in this post will thank you for your work. The ones living off the system will continue to fall in step with your attempt at censorship

> Comedy is usually based in reality.....call it racist if you must....not too far off from the truth (I didn't write this one but it IS funny and scary at the same time)

The above justifications only further exacerbated the county GOP's problems and the party soon went into retreat and apology mode. Towle issued a statement that contained a more comprehensive apology, though even this one limited who it was addressed to:

"I totally regret that some members of the Democratic Party were offended by the satirical post on this page yesterday. There were some that commented on the post that they did not see how the possibly inflammatory comments were anything other than political commentary. This page is not the original author and the intent was to show the author's frustration at the current economic situation that he/she finds themselves in.

I realize now that there are those that were deeply offended and for that I am very saddened and I will make sure that our editorial process will result in posts to our pages that reflect the spirit of good natured political discussions. My hope is that we can get back to the critical dialog necessary to move Vermont and the US back towards economic prosperity."

Towle expanded on his apology the next day, saying in an interview that, "I realized that it was inappropriate and insensitive and I'm truly sorry for having posted it in the first place." Towle was then forced to issue another statement with an even broader apology the next day. "It was a case of bad judgment and anyone that knows me, knows that the post does not reflect my personal values, nor does it in any way reflect the values or beliefs of any GOP official, candidate, GOP worker, or any person that I am friends with or associate with."

Naturally, Democrats used the incident to hit the Republican Party. Jake Perkinson, head of the Vermont Democratic Party, called the comments "vile and disgusting" and used the opportunity to highlight earlier comments made by Maine's governor, Paul

LePage, in which LePage compared the IRS to the Nazi Gestapo. Thus, Towle's comments gave the Democratic Party another opportunity to rehash earlier regretful comments and further paint the Republican Party as extremists.

At this point the story had gone national, appearing on Huffington Post, NBC News and the *Washington Post*. By July 17, the GOP Rutland Facebook page had been deleted.

None of this helped the Republican Party of Vermont in 2012:

- President Obama shellacked Mitt Romney, defeating him 67-31 percent and winning Rutland by a 60-38 percent margin.

- Socialist Bernie Sanders, who caucuses with the Democrats in the Senate, easily crushed his GOP opponent, winning reelection 71-25 percent.

- Vermont's Congressman Peter Welch (D) was reelected 72-23 percent.

- Governor Peter Shumlin (D) was easily reelected, Randy Brock (R) 57-38 percent.
- Vermont Democrats gained four seats in the state House of Representatives, increasing their margin over Republicans to 98-43, with eight members of other parties and one vacancy.

- Vermont Democrats picked up one seat in their Senate, increasing their margin over

Republicans to 21-7, with two members of other parties.

The Lesson:

- Training and guidelines are necessary: As this story demonstrates, everyone in an organization who has access to social media must receive training about its proper use. A general policy should be in place that spells out what can and cannot be said. For politicians and elected officials, that policy should also dictate what content is responded to, ignored or deleted.

- Control who has the keys: Clearly, not everyone in a group should be given access to social media. In some cases, it pays for an organization to be selective in who has the keys. Of course, you can't exactly tell the head of an organization that they can't use Facebook or tweet. In that case, try to emphasize training as much as possible or simply get the responsibility delegated to one person – and one person only.

- Don't make conditional apologies: Towle's apology is a great example of how not to apologize. Notice that, at one point, he apologized to "some members of the Democratic Party" who he offended. Of course, this statement is ridiculous. Anyone with a sense of decency should have been offended by the joke, not just "some members of the Democratic Party." When you apologize, do so without reservation, not just to "some people" who might have been offended.

Chapter Thirty-five:

Power hungry angry black man

The Background: In January 2010, Mike Parry (@mikeparry) won a special election to fill a vacancy in Minnesota's 26th State Senate District. Parry made it clear that he wouldn't be a standard politician. Upon winning the endorsement of the Republican Party for the 26th Senate District, he told delegates that, "like them, he wants 'a Senator that is not worried about being politically correct.'"

The Fail: Parry decided to use Twitter in a method that can be safely described as the polar opposite of political correctness. First, there's this tweet about Obama being an arrogant black man:

> read the exclusive on Mr. O in Newsweek. He is a Power Hungry Arrogant Black Man

Parry also seemed concerned about absentee ballot voter fraud but had no conception of how absentee balloting actually worked:

Only those in service overseas can vote absentee!

Stop Absentee Voter Fraud

This actually isn't a true statement. In Minnesota, anyone who is not present in their precinct, is sick, serving as an election judge or observing a religious holiday can vote via absentee. Last, and probably most offensive, was this tweet:

whats with the Dems and Pedophiles?

The tweet occurred after the passage of the Matthew Shepard and James Byrd, Jr. Hate Crimes Prevention Act, which expanded the definition of a hate crime to crimes related to gender, sexual orientation, gender identification or disability.

The Response and Consequences: At first, Parry tried to blame his opponents for confusing his message and distracting people from the "real issues." When confronted by the media, Parry said, "My opinion is that our president is arrogant and angry. The fact is that he is a black man. Now if the Democratic Party and the liberals want to take my opinion and the fact and mix it together and use it to bring a bad light about me and keep them away from discussing the real issues they can do that all they want. They're grasping for straws." What about the tweet that linked Democrats and pedophiles? "If it's on my account, I wouldn't know how that one got there...I don't remember reading anything that would connect me making a statement like that...I would have to have read something that would have created me making a statement like that."

In the end, Parry did what any political candidate not concerned with political correctness would do: He scrubbed his twitter account, deleting 33 tweets.

In 2010, Parry was fortunate. He had no opponent in the general election and was reelected. Two years later, sought the Republican nomination to run for Congress in Minnesota's 1st Congressional District and lost that race to Republican Allen Quist by a 54-45 percent margin. Parry's controversial statements and positions certainly didn't help him win this race and his unsuccessful congressional run ended his political career.

The Lesson:

- Watch what you claim: Obviously, Parry's tweets were offensive and repulsive. What was perhaps most bizarre about Parry's tweets was his initial claims of being a senator who didn't care about political correctness. Fair enough. But if you don't care about political correctness, don't get busted deleting tweets.

Chapter Thirty-six:

Are you Asian? Then you must be Chinese and shipping jobs overseas.

The Background: Progress Kentucky (@ProgressKy) was formed in December 2011 with one goal: to elect a new senator to the seat currently occupied by Mitch McConnell (R-KY), then the Senate Minority Leader. McConnell had served as Kentucky's senator since 1985 and as Republican Senate Leader since 2007. Since 1993, McConnell has been married to Elaine Chao. Chao served as Secretary of Labor under George W. Bush and was the first Asian American to ever serve in a U.S. cabinet.

The Fail: In mid to late February 2012, Progress Kentucky issued a series of racist tweets. The first came on February 14:

This woman has the ear of @McConnellPress – she's his #wife. May explain why your job moved to China! rense.com/general77/raci...

The link took readers to a website hosted by radio show host Jeff Rense. Rense alleged that Chao discriminated against American workers while Secretary of Labor. Among other allegations featured on Rense's website: proposals to attack Syria are just a Zionist plot, Barack Obama was behind a terrorist attack on a mall in Kenya, and the newest evidence yet of hidden photographs that showcase aliens in Roswell.

Four more racially charged tweets were issued between February 23-26:

I think you'd have to go to NY NJ TX & China to find the people #MitchMcConnell represents! @ McConnellPress

More non-Kentuckians #BUYING our election? Chao family gives very big to #KyRepublican Party shar.es/Ydp7C @McConnellPress

FYI: @Team_Mitch father-in-law is shipbuilding industrialist to whom Chinese Premier Wen Jiabao #grateful ow.ly/i2Qjv

China Premier grateful to McConnell father-in-law/@ KYGOP contributor-4 his role in developing China industry ow.ly/i2Qjv #kyga13

The Response and Consequences: The stupidity of these tweets exists on so many different levels. First, McConnell's wife was born in Taiwan, not China, and moved to the United States when she was eight. Second, someone being from Asia does not automatically mean that they are trying to outsource American jobs. Third, there are plenty of ways to make a politically potent argument without being blatantly racist.

McConnell's campaign condemned the statement and used the opportunity to attack Progress Kentucky. Jesse Benton, McConnell's campaign manager, said, "We just think this kind of race-baiting has absolutely no place in American politics. We think Progress Kentucky should really be ashamed of what's been going out under their name. People should be fired and a public apology should be issued. I think everybody of good conscience in Kentucky should agree that these sorts of attacks should be pushed to the side."

The statements earned universal condemnations from some of McConnell's biggest foes. The Kentucky Democratic Party said that Progress Kentucky's tweets were "deplorable and have absolutely no place in Kentucky." Ashley Judd (@ashleyjudd), who was rumored to be a possible candidate against McConnell at the time, also condemned the tweets:

Whatever the intention, whatever the venue, whomever the person, the attacks or comments on anyone's ethnicity are wrong & patently unacceptable.

At first, Progress Kentucky dug in. "Senator Mitch McConnell has a conflict of interest that many are afraid to talk about, and Progress Kentucky is not." In a later statement on February 26, Chris Morrison of Progress Kentucky gave a half apology, acknowledging that some tweets may "have crossed the line" but still adding that "it's fair to question whether or not there's a conflict of interest." This marginal apology was a terrible strategy and Progress Kentucky was eventually forced to backtrack. Later on February 26, Progress Kentucky Executive Director Shawn Reilly acknowledged that the tweets in question "included an inappropriate comment on the ethnicity" of Chao. "We apologize to the Secretary for that unnecessary comment and have deleted the tweets in question. In addition, we have put a review process in place to ensure tweets and other social media communications from Progress Kentucky are reviewed and approved prior to posting."

In April 2013, things only got worse for Progress Kentucky when it came to light that the group was behind the secret recording of a conversation between McConnell and aides that detailed how they planned on attacking Ashley Judd, as well as other possible Democratic candidates. Recording someone without their consent is a crime, and doing so to a powerful U.S. senator is even worse. The FBI was called to investigate.

Ultimately, the multitude of scandals was too much for the organization to overcome. In August 2013, the FEC approved the closing of Progress Kentucky at the request of the organization itself.

The Lesson:

- When you are in a hole, quit digging: When you do something stupid, an apology is almost always the best path forward. It's hard and it involves a pretty big hit to the ego, but it is usually the right thing, and the best thing, to do. At a bare minimum, don't defend conduct that is obviously reprehensible and don't brag about being one of the few organizations that is "willing" to bring up topics. When you are in a hole, stop digging. Apologize completely and openly. Then move on.

- Don't distract from your message: As the liberal website Think Progress (no relation to Progress Kentucky) noted, "There are legitimate reasons to criticize Chao's tenure as Labor Secretary; her heritage has nothing to do with them." Like many senators, McConnell has amassed a voting record that has left him open to attacks that he has supported the outsourcing of jobs overseas. The ample evidence could have provided an open line of attack for groups like Progress Kentucky. Instead, they chose to attack McConnell's wife for being Chinese (and again, she was actually born in Taiwan, an entirely different country and ethnicity). The point is that if you have a valid line of attack, use it, and use it clearly. Don't confuse the issue by taking racist shots at your opponent's wife.

- Don't attack the family: When it comes to political attacks, most things are no longer considered out of bounds in American politics. However, barring extreme ethical misconduct that is obviously connected to the candidate, don't attack someone's spouse or family. It's tactless and almost always backfires. The average voter will, more likely than not, emphasize with the candidate and realize that they wouldn't want anyone attacking their family. Why should some politician be any different? By and large, family remains one of the few things that is still (thankfully) off-limits. Candidates for office would be wise to adhere to this rule.

Chapter Thirty-seven:

How many racist comments can you cram into two tweets?

The Background: Jenniffer Gonzalez was the Speaker of the House of Representatives of Puerto Rico. She had served in that capacity since 2008 and as a Representative since 2002. She is also a member of the New Progressive Party of Puerto Rico which, despite its name, is affiliated with the Republican Party. One of Gonzales's advisers was Heidi Wys (@HeidiWys), who served Gonzalez as an Administrative Consultant. Wys had worked for Gonzalez since 2008 and earned over $630,000 in her position as of August 2012.

The Fail: Wys issued two tweets that were ignorant, xenophobic and blatantly racist. First, on June 18, 2012, in response to a dinner contest issued by President Obama's twitter account, Wys responded with:

> @BarackObama Wah! Wah! I feel like vomiting! Dinner with a guy borned in Kenya and claims he was borned in Hawaii!

Then, on July 26, 2012, President Obama tweeted a note about Michelle Obama's upcoming birthday. Wys responded with the following:

@BarackObama Who cares? Take her to Burger King, buy her a sundae with a double banana, take her to your homeland, Kenya!!

Within the space of 140 characters, Wys simultaneously made a racist crack about the Obamas having similarities to monkeys (a common insult against blacks) and a reference to the completely debunked theory of Obama being born in Kenya. You have to give her credit: That's a lot of hate to cram into one tweet.

The Response and Consequences: Stories on the tweets first appeared on July 30. Wys originally responded to the controversy by tweeting that she wasn't racist, just opposed to the president. "Journalists who want to make an 'issue' out of my comment about Obama. I am not racist. My favorite nieces are dark-skinned! I'm Anti-Obama. I'm against him."

Unsurprisingly, the quotes did nothing to tamper down the reaction against Wys. "How is it that Puerto Rico 'does it better' [Puerto Rico's tourism slogan] if the government pays an employee who is discriminating against the President of the United States? This is placing the name of Puerto Ricans across the world in a very precarious situation," said Puerto Rica Senator Juan Eugenio Hernandez. Rafael Cox Alomar, a candidate for Puerto Rico's resident commissioner (representative in U.S. Congress), added that, "no one should underestimate the grave affront that a racial attack represents, using political differences as an excuse."

Among those condemning Wys' tweets: Puerto Rico's favorite son, Ricky Martin (@Ricky_martin):

@Heidiwys It's one thing to have political differences but another to exhibit racism and xenophobia. Your comments are regrettable and unacceptable.

Beyond Wys' initial tweet, neither she nor Jenniffer Gonzalez gave any immediate statement, which allowed their political opposition to continue to attack. Gonzalez responded three days after the first story on the tweets appeared. In the statement, she condemned the remarks: "The expressions disseminated are not acceptable, do not represent my sentiments and are the exclusive responsibility of those who wrote them." However, at the same time, Gonzalez noted that she couldn't monitor the social media of her entire staff. Apparently, Gonzalez didn't have any policies in place that would make it clear that racist tweets against the President are unacceptable.

Later the same day (August 2) Wys issued an apology over Twitter, in Spanish. Translated, Wys said, "I regret that the tweets made to B. Obama were perceived as racist. My intention was to attack a politician whom I don't believe in. In light of the fact that the House Speaker has been unjustly attacked, I want to distance her and the House from these incidents. The tweets were done in my personal character and from home. I apologize to those who were offended. I fight Obama the politician, not the person." Wys then proceeded to delete the original tweets and protect her account, making it impossible to be viewed by anyone who wasn't already following her and allowing no one else to be able to follow her without approval.

Ultimately, Gonzalez did not remove Wys from her position, but it didn't matter. In the 2012 elections, the Popular Democratic Party overtook the New Progressive Party in Puerto Rico's House of Representatives. As a result, Gonzalez was removed from office as Speaker, though she remained a member of the House.

As for Wys, she is no longer on Twitter. She deleted her account.

The Lesson:

- Don't couch the apology: Both Gonzalez and Wys are guilty of sending out half-hearted apologies. Gonzalez made sure to apologize but added that she couldn't monitor her staff's social media. No one expects that. What people do expect is for politicians to take responsibility for heinous social media usage by their staffers. Unfair? Maybe. But that's not the point. Wys, of course, apologized to anyone offended and for the fact that her tweets were "perceived" as racist. First, there was no perception problem; they were blatantly racist. Second, you never apologize to anyone offended; you apologize to everyone, including the person you wronged, the President. Indeed, Gonzalez should have called the White House to apologize and stated as such. Regardless, the point is this. When you apologize, make it a full one. Don't give half-hearted apologies.

- Speed kills: The stories on the racist tweets broke on July 30; neither Gonzalez nor Wys responded until August 2. This gave the political opposition plenty of time to attack both Gonzalez and Wys, and attack they did. Meanwhile, with no cohesive response, stories filled the airways that did NOT have an apology or any statement of regret. In a scandal, speed kills. Responses have to be quicker than three days.

Chapter Thirty-eight:

C'Mon N' Ride It

The Background: In 2010, Republican Scott Walker was a candidate for governor in Wisconsin. A hot issue in the race was Walker's opposition to a proposed high speed rail that would run between Madison and Milwaukee. The proposal as supported by President Obama and by Walker's Democratic opponent, Tom Barrett, the mayor of Milwaukee. On August 16, President Obama stumped in Wisconsin with Barrett.

Also involved in this screw-up were two Walker staffers: Jill Bader, Walker's communications director, and Michael Brickman, a press assistant for Walker.

The Fail: On August 16, the day of Obama's visit with Barrett, Brickman (@BrickM) sent out a tweet that linked to "Pres. Obama's response" to Scott Walker's opposition of the proposed rail line. That tweet was then retweeted by Bader (@Jillbader).

The tweet contained a link that Bader thought went to a blog entry by the *Hot Air Blog*. However, it actually directed users to a YouTube video for Quad Ciy DJ's C'mon'n Ride It (The Train), as performed on the TV Show *Soul Train*.

QuadCity DJs was an entirely African-American group and *Soul Tra*in featured mostly African-American bands. Indeed, the video itself features dancers that are almost exclusively black. The racial undertones here – showing a video of entirely black people in response to a black president – were hard to miss.

The Response and Consequences: Bader deleted the tweet and apologized the same day:

> I apologize. Was just alerted my RT wasn't what I thought it was – here is what I thought was sending @hotairblog: http://bit.ly/913VYs

That link actually went to the blog Hot Air and showed a one minute video of Walker attacking Obama for the proposed rail line.

While Bader did apologize, Brickman never did, and the controversy extended up to Walker. A Wisconsin radio reporter called it "the story of the day" and Tom Barrett said that he thought the Walker campaign should apologize, adding that he thought it was pretty obvious that the tweet was, in fact, intentional. "Not one, but two Walker staffers sent it around, and that leads me to conclude that it was not an accident...I think they should just admit that it was tasteless and apologize." Surrogates for Barrett also went on the attack. In a press conference, State

Senator Lena Taylor (D-Milwaukee), an African-American, attacked the tweets, calling them "distasteful and disrespectful."

Walker's campaign issued a brief statement of apology later that day. "An honest mistake was made by a staffer that forwarded a message from a blogger that linked to a video rather than a blog post. When it was brought to our attention, she immediately removed the message and apologized to anyone that was offended by it."

Keith Olbermann, who was still hosting his show on MSNBC at the time, named Jill Bader his "Worst Person in the World" for the tweet, bringing it to national attention. It was certainly a distraction for Walker, who at the time was campaigning against the Democratic Party and Obama's damaged brand. He wanted to talk about jobs and the economy, not race.

In the end, it didn't matter. Scott Walker beat Barrett 52-46 percent. Walker did, in fact, refuse the aid for the high speed rail and the money was split among 13 other states.

Incidentally, this wouldn't be Brickman's last media controversy of the campaign. He got into more trouble when he posted a satirical version of Walker's jobs plan to Walker's campaign blog. The plan made fun of Barrett's jobs plan by using a huge font to describe Walkers' and make it one page longer than Barrett's. Barrett attacked the post, noting that it was offensive to joke about jobs at a time when so many were unemployed.

The Lesson:

- Be as careful as humanly possible: Did Brickman or Bader have any racist intentions when they sent out the tweet, or was it an accidental link, as Bader said? There was never a clear answer on that, though the evidence seems to imply that at least Brickman knew what he was doing. After all, there was a "Ha!" in the original tweet and the link that she claimed she was trying to direct people to wasn't funny at all. However, it is certainly possible that all she was trying to do was mock the president's rail policies with a goofy music video. If that was the case, Bader is guilty of another crime: not being as cautious as she should have been. As has been said throughout this book, the standards are higher for people who are seeking or holding elected office, as well as their staff. Bader should have realized that the use of a music video from a primarily African-American show, combined with almost entirely African-American dancers, would leave her open to charges of racism.

- Watch your links: Assuming for a moment that Bader was telling the truth about the accidental retweet, there is a lesson here as well: watch your links. Always double check a link that you are tweeting out. After all, you would never forward an email without reading it first. Nor would you vouch for a person who you had never met. Why would you retweet a link without checking it first?

- Apologize and be quick: Bader did one thing right here: she apologized extremely quickly as soon as she realized what had happened and offered an explanation.

Chapter Thirty-nine:

Per the Republican Party, racism is over

The Background: On December 1, 1955, Rosa Parks refused to vacate a bus seat for a white man, as was required at the time. Her arrest ultimately led to the Montgomery Bus Boycott and was an important victory for civil rights and anti-segregation efforts in the South. Parks ultimately became a powerful icon against racism and segregation.

The Fail: On December 1, 2013, the 58th anniversary of Parks' civil disobedience and arrest, the national Republican Party (@GOP) sent out this tweet:

Today we remember Rosa Parks' bold stand and her role in ending racism.

The tweet also contained a picture of Parks, along with one of her most famous quotes: "You must never be fearful about what you are doing when it is right."

The tweet itself contained the words "ending racism," as if racism has been completely removed from society. This probably came as news to every racial minority, as polls as recent as 2012 show that a majority of Americans express prejudice, while at least one-third of Hispanics have experienced racism within the past five years.

The Response: The errand tweet came as Republicans were attempting to accelerate their outreach efforts towards racial minorities. In the 2012 elections, Mitt Romney was absolutely shellacked by President Obama among African Americans (93-6%) and Hispanics (69-29%). Accordingly, the party had invested serious time and money at boosting their standing within these groups. In March 2013, a post-election GOP report indicated that Republicans had to increase their racial outreach efforts in order to be competitive in the future. In August, the party launched a program to increase the visibility of its female and minority "rising stars." In October, Republicans had hired their first state staff whose sole responsibility was minority outreach. That effort, in North Carolina, then spread to New Jersey, Virginia and Michigan.

To that end, it's safe to say that the tweet undercut Republican efforts to engage minorities.

The tweet was widely mocked in liberal circles and in the mainstream media. The incident was covered in by CNN, Huffington Post, Buzzfeed and NPR, among other outlets.

As is essentially standard operating procedure, Twitter users were quick to turn the GOP's misguided tweet into a funny hashtag. In this case, #RacismEndedWhen became the central location of countless satirical tweets, including:

> @redstmiscreant: #RacismEndedWhen Confederate President Abraham Lincoln freed the slaves from Yankee oppression during the War of Northern Aggression.

> @bluesharque: #RacismEndedWhen the GOP began to suppress EVERYBODY'S vote!

> @chimezie: #RacismEndedWhen Rick Perry turned down #ACA Medicaid expansion to cover poor folks with no access to healthcare.

Four hours after the initial tweet was sent, the GOP issued a correction:

Previous tweet should have read "Today we remember Rosa Parks' bold stand and her role in fighting to end racism."

The Lesson:

- Speed kills: Four hours isn't much time, but it's an eternity in the universe of social media and national politics. The Republican Party has a full-time staff dedicated towards managing their significant social media presence. As such, there is no excuse for such a long delay. This should not have taken four hours. This should have taken less than two, if that. The extended time frame gave this incident a chance to spread when a quicker response could have helped kill its momentum.

- Phrasing matters: From a purely linguistics perspective, there isn't a huge difference between "her role in ending racism" and "her role in fighting to end racism." Really, it's only a difference of three words. Of course, in politics, it's all the difference in the world. As you have seen and will see throughout this book, single words, even single letters, can mean the difference between message success and failure. Choose what you say carefully.

- You will never get the benefit of the doubt: In all fairness, it's doubtful that there are many Republicans who truly believe that racism is over. Still, this incident illustrates a simple social media truth: Politicians and political parties will never get the benefit of the doubt from their opponents. Democrats didn't hesitate to join the pile on against the GOP when the first tweet broke and Republicans most certainly wouldn't hesitate if the shoe were on the other foot. To that end, in politics, it's foolish to expect your opponents to let a softball go by. Do not expect the benefit of the doubt from the political opposition.

Chapter Forty:

British Member of Parliament uses racial slur and is threatened with police investigation

The Background: Jack Dromey (@JackDromeyMP) is a British Member of Parliament and has been since 2010. He comes from a politically connected family: his wife, Harriet Harman, is the Deputy Leader of the Labor Party. Dromey managed to have three social media scandals in 2013. In September, he favorited a tweet that contained a link to a gay porn website. Then in November, he accidentally sent out a link that contained similar material. Spokesmen said both incidents occurred when Dromey pressed the wrong button while trying to block the tweets. Making the incidents more embarrassing is that Dromey's wife had campaigned against pornography.

The Fail: On December 13, 2013, while on a visit to a Royal Mail facility in his constituency, Dromey sent out the following tweet:

With Gareth Martin, the Pikey from the Erdington Royal Mail Sorting Office. A great guy!

The tweet featured a picture of Dromey with Martin. The controversy here came from the use of the word pikey. Pikey is a slang, pejorative term that refers to iterant travelers. Many within the Irish and Romanian community consider it to be an ethnic slur.

The Response and Consequences: After the initial negative response, Dromey sent out the following:

Don't panic, Mr Mainwaring. The morning's meeting was with Gareth, a Postie nicknamed after Corporal Pike from Dad's Army @GuidoFawkes

Dad's Army was a British TV show that aired from 1968-1977 and featured a character named Colonel Pike. The Royal Mail, however, was quick to deny that such a nickname was in use, with a spokesperson saying, "I can confirm there is no such slang term for a role within Royal Mail delivery offices."

It only got worse for Dromey. He received hundreds of complaints about the tweet, with users calling it disgraceful, disgustingly insulting and racist. Even worse is that, since 2007, it has been illegal to use the term "pikey" in Britain. David Morris, a member of the Tory Party (and rivals to Dromey's Labour Party) asked the Metropolitan Police Commissioner to launch an inquiry into the incident. Such an investigation never occurred: even Gareth

Martin, the man who is supposedly nicknamed Pikey, called Dromey a "top bloke" and close personal friend while confirming that the use of "pikey" was a nickname. Regardless, the entire incident was a black eye for Dromey, who should have known better than to use a racial slur in a tweet, regardless of the context.

The Lesson:

- Be aware of double meanings: Given the meaning of the word "pikey," Dromey should never have sent this tweet. Even Dromey's Labour Party said that their members should be more careful with their tweets. After the incident, a Labour Party spokesman said, "It is an offensive word and it just shows how everybody should be extremely careful with language on Twitter." As the *British Express Star* correctly noted, "What's really surprising, in this sensitive, politically-correct age, is that any MP would dream of using the word 'pikey,' no matter what the context, and then be surprised when all hell broke loose."

- Know how to use Twitter: Virtually every story about the pikey scandal referred to Dromey's previous social media disasters with tweets containing links to gay porn. As such, these incidents further eroded Dromey's credibility. Surely, Dromey's foul-ups had many wondering how he could possibly govern if he couldn't even manage a Twitter account. To that end, make sure you fully understand the platform that you are using, lest you fall victim to an embarrassing mistake.

Chapter Forty-one:

I will choke that illegal Mex

The Background: Taylor Palmisano (@itstaytime), 23, worked as the Deputy Finance Director for Scott Walker's gubernatorial campaign. In November 2013, Palmisano wrote an email to Walker supporters, encouraging them to donate to the governor, instead of buying "electronics or toys that will undoubtedly be outdated, broken or lost by the next Holiday Season."

The Fail: In December 2013, No Quarter, an investigative column run by Daniel Bice of the *Wisconsin Journal Sentinel*, discovered these two tweets from Palmisano's personal account:

I will choke that illegal mex cleaning in the library. Stop banging fucking chairs around and turn off your Walkman. (3/9/11)

This bus is my worst fucking nightmare Nobody speaks English & these ppl dont know how 2 control their kids #only3morehours #illegalalients (1/3/11)

The Response and Consequences: Palmisano was fired immediately. In a statement, Walker spokesman Jonathan Wetzel said, "Taylor Palmisano has been immediately removed from her position with the Friends of Scott Walker campaign. Both the governor, and the campaign, condemn these insulting remarks which do not reflect our views in any way." In her own statement, Palmisano expressed regret and took responsibility for her actions, saying, "I deeply regret these offensive and irresponsible remarks. I sincerely apologize, and understand the consequences of making such unacceptable statements."

Making matters worse for Walker was that this was the third scandal involving racist actions and his staff. In addition to the "Ride the Train" tweet (see Chapter Five), in August 2013, another Walker staffer had to be fired due to racist online comments. Steven Kreisser, who was serving as the Assistant Secretary of State for the Wisconsin Department of Transportation, took to Facebook to blast immigrants, saying that, "You may see Jesus when you look at them. I see Satan" while calling immigrants a "stream of wretched criminals" that had ruined entire states and industries. Like Palmisano, Kreisser was immediately fired.

Even more embarrassing: Walker was among the Republicans who was actively encouraging his own party to better engage with minority communities, telling Bloomberg in August 2012 that he felt Republicans should better connect with minorities by emphasizing small business issues, while deemphasizing immigration.

The Lesson:

- How recently doesn't matter: By the time they were discovered, Palmisano's comments were more than two and a half years old. For all anyone knew, she could have made remarkable progress as a person during that time and had grown past her prior racist comments and views. From a career and public relations perspective, timeliness doesn't matter at all. Palmisano paid a deep price for older comments and that's a powerful lesson: Time does not, in fact, heal all wounds.

- Background check the staff: As noted, this was Walker's third scandal involving the racist comments of his staffers. Clearly, Walker's administration needs to conduct a more intensive search into the background of employees. Indeed, when you play at a level as high as Governor Walker, who is also viewed as a likely 2016 Presidential contender, it is essentially a requirement. That being said, consult your HR department before you start looking up the Facebook profile of a job candidate. Depending on what you are hiring for and what information you learn and your hiring decision, you may be subjecting yourself to a lawsuit.

Chapter Forty-two:

Let's shoot the protestors

The Background: In February 2011, Wisconsin was roiled in an incredibly passionate debate about collective bargaining rights of public employees. Pro-union protestors were flooding the Capital in Madison. At the time, Jeff Cox (@JCCentCom) was a deputy attorney general for the neighboring State of Indiana.

The Fail: This tweet, from Cox:

Use live ammunition RT @MotherJones Sources in Madison say riot police have been ordered to clear protestors from capitol at 2 am #wiunion

The Response and Consequences: When confronted over his behavior by a reporter for Mother Jones, Cox referred to demonstrators as "political enemies" and "thugs." But did he really advocate for deadly force? "You're damned right I advocate deadly force," said Cox. In addition to the ill-advised tweet, Cox also ran a blog where he compared political opponents to Nazis, expressed his support for police who beat up a black teenager and advocated for a policy in Afghanistan that consisted of, "KILL! KILL!"

Cox was fired. In a press release, the Indiana Attorney General's office stated: "Civility and courtesy toward all members of the public are very important to the Indiana Attorney General's Office. We respect individuals' First Amendment right to express their personal views on private online forums; but as public servants we are held by the public to a higher standard and we should strive for civility."

The Lesson:

- Advocating for deadly force against peaceful protestors is bad: Apparently, this needs to be stated. This should really be common sense: don't advocate to kill a group of protestors who happen to disagree with you.

- Check your Social Media policy: Cox most certainly ran afoul of his office's social media policy, which laid out standards of behavior for employees. This helps to drive home an important point in the public and private sector: know what your expectations are when it comes to social media. Even social media use on your own time can potentially get you into hot water, a lesson that Jeff Cox learned the hard way.

Chapter Forty-three:

Isn't domestic violence a hoot?

The Background: In February 2013, at a hearing on a domestic violence case, New Hampshire State Representative Mark Warden (R-Manchester) commented that, "Some people could make the argument that a lot of people like being in abusive relationships. It's a love-hate relationship." The comment, predictably, was condemned by anti-domestic violence organizations, Democrats and even the state Republican Party. Warden would later apologize for the remark, saying it was never his intention to "minimize the trauma of domestic abuse." But naturally, people didn't forget about the comments.

One of Warden's defenders was fellow State Representative Kyle Tasker (R-Nottingham). Tasker is no stranger to controversy. In previous social media posts, he joked that he needed to drink before meeting with Democrats and posted videos implying that African-American women are unfit mothers. In

2012, during a public safety panel hearing, Tasker dropped one of his loaded guns.

The Fail: Fast forward to February 2014. The incident about Warden's comments was being discussed on the Nashua Party Tea Party Facebook page, with some members attacking and others defending Warden's comment. Representative Tasker (R-Nottingham) was one of Warden's defenders, commenting that, "Warden is so principled it offends people." And then, this astounding post:

When another commenter noted that the post was inappropriate, Tasker responded, "Nahh. I ran it by the [domestic violence] lobbyist she laughed. Now if we went around wearing the T-shirt that wouldn't go over well."

The Response and Consequences: Naturally, Tasker's absurd post turned into a national story on outlets like Talking Points Memo and Huffington Post. Among those condemning him was the New

Hampshire Republican Party, which was forced to refute the remarks of one of its own members for the second time in a year. In a statement, Jennifer Horn, the chairwoman of the New Hampshire Republican Party, said, "Representative Tasker's post was grossly offensive and has no place in public discourse. He should apologize immediately."

Tasker did delete the post, but he refused to apologize for it, opting instead to say that the post was simply misconstrued. "The idea was to show something pretty outrageous to put (Rep. Warden's) comments in perspective."

The Lesson:

- Watch your defense: Representative Tasker was trying to defend what he saw as an unjust attack on a colleague and friend. This is an admirable intention, but there are two problems with what he did. First, he picked something pretty indefensible. It's difficult, if not impossible, to defend the comments that Representative Warden made in the first place – no woman ever "likes" being in an abusive relationship, and even Warden himself apologized for the comments. Second, the manner in which Tasker chose to defend his friend was utterly absurd. He chose to try to defend one gaffe by making an even bigger gaffe. This is the equivalent of dealing with a sprained wrist by taking a sledgehammer to your ankle. If you want to defend a friend, that's one thing, but you can't do so by intentionally putting yourself in the line of fire.

Chapter Forty-four:

Don't wish death on someone's children

The Background: Amanda Carpenter (@amandacarpenter) serves as a speechwriter and senior communications advisor to Senator Ted Cruz (R-TX), a Tea Party favorite. At the time of the fail, Allan Brauer (@allanbrauer) served as the communications director for the Sacramento Democratic Party.

The Fail: In September 2013, Carpenter tweeted her confident belief that the GOP could be victorious in their efforts to defund Obamacare:

> GOP beat gun control, changed Obama's mind on Syria, is holding the line on amnesty. We can defund Obamacare, too!

Allan Brauer responded with this:

> @amandacarpenter May your children all die from debilitating, painful and incurable diseases.

The astounding tweet violated almost every rule of politics and social media: from invoking death to attacking someone's children, the tweet couldn't have gotten much worse - until it did. Carpenter retweeted Brauer's comments and added "Deserves some unfollows." Brauer then sent out two more tweets:

> Busy blocking the tapeworms that have slithered out of hellspawn @amandacarpenter's asshole. How's your day so far?

> I'm being attacked on Twitter for wishing one of Ted Cruz's pubic lice to experience the pain her boss is inflicting on Americans.

The Response and Consequences: Cruz's office did not respond to a request for a comment. Carpenter herself sent out a memorable response that just any parent can sympathize with:

> Now I have the pleasure of notifying my husband a California Democrat wished death on our kids. Sigh.

The apology from Brauer came within two hours of the first tweet:

> Hi @amandacarpenter I am truly sorry for my tweet. I was very upset and lashed out. Your kids are not fair game either. My apologies.

To her infinite credit, Carpenter very graciously accepted.

Even worse, at least from a PR perspective, is that Brauer's tweets gave conservatives more ammunition against Democrats. Brauer's tweets were picked up on by conservative news outlets like Fox News and Breitbart.

The apology was not even close to saving Brauer's volunteer position. The Sacramento Democratic Party asked for and received Brauer's resignation. In a statement, Kerri Asbury, Chair of the Sacramento Democratic Party, said, "The comments by our volunteer communications chair are appalling and inexcusable. No matter what our political disagreements may be, wishing harm is never an acceptable response during heated public debate or any other time. Mr. Brauer has apologized for his comments and expressed his remorse."

It is worth noting that the original tweet and subsequent resignation came on the same day, September 20. The Sacramento Democratic Party deserves credit for moving extremely quickly to deal with the situation.

The Lesson:

- Set guidelines for volunteers: As this incident demonstrated, some sort of policy is needed for volunteers. In the case of someone like Brauer, it might not have even made a difference. Even the best policy can be ignored if those whom it is supposed to govern choose to discard it. However, this is a case study in why social media policies are necessary for employees and volunteers who represent your organization.

Chapter FORTY-five:

This is not how you win women voters

The Background: Alison Lundergan Grimes is the elected Secretary of State in Kentucky. In July 2013, Grimes announced that she would challenge incumbent Senator Mitch McConnell in the 2014 U.S. Senate election. A December 2013, a poll showed her down by a mere point to McConnell, vaulting her to top tier status among Democrats seeking to unseat Republican senators. McConnell, meanwhile, enjoyed widespread support from all levels of Republican campaign machinery. One of the most critical cogs in that machine is the National Republican Senate Committee (@NRSC), the campaign arm of Senate Republicans.

The Fail: On November 19, 2013, the NRSC sent out this tweet:

Is Alison Grimes Is the New "Obama Girl"?
bluegrassbulletin.com/2013/11/grimes...
#KYSEN via @mercuscarey

The tweet itself is a reference to the Obama Girl videos, from 2007, which featured a sexy model singing about her crush on then Senator Obama. Unsurprisingly, the tweet attempted to link Grimes to Obama, who was very unpopular in Kentucky. However, the article it actually links to includes this horrendously photoshopped picture:

The face is Grimes on the body of a model wearing an Obama shirt. This is obviously not a good way to woo women voters. Even worse, the tweet was retweeted by Iris Wilbur, McConnell's political director.

This was not the first time that the NRSC had made sexist comments about Grimes. Early in 2013, Brad Dayspring, the organization's communications director, referred to Grimes as an "empty dress" while comparing her to a nervous high school student, adding that Grimes "babbles incoherently and stares blankly into the camera as though she's a freshman in high school struggling to remember the CliffsNotes after forgetting to read her homework assignment."

The Response and Consequences: In a statement, Grimes blasted the tweet and the picture: "The NRSC should stand for Notoriously Repeating Sexist Comments – they cannot relate or connect with the women of Kentucky or our country. The incredibly inappropriate comments from Senator McConnell's team mark a developing pattern and demonstrate just how out of touch McConnell is with the women of Kentucky."

To its credit, the NRSC quickly admitted its mistake. NRSC spokeswoman Brook Hougesen called the tweet "extremely offensive" and threw the staffer who had sent the tweet under the campaign bus; "It was a mistake made by a junior staffer and disciplinary action has been taken. We took corrective action as soon as it was brought to our attention and have taken steps to ensure it will never happen again." Both the tweet and the blog entry were deleted.

The Lesson:

- Train your staff: Assume, for a moment, that the NRSC's explanation is accurate and that this tweet was sent out by a junior staffer who didn't know any better. If this was true, the NRSC is still to blame: their social media policies and training were clearly inadequate. Anyone involved in campaigns knows that you have to fall over yourself to avoid saying or doing anything that stinks of racism or sexism. Clearly, the offending staffer missed that lesson. Make sure your staff is competent enough to avoid committing mistakes like this. More to the point, have a list of content that should always be avoided. Sexist and racist material should be at the top of that list.

- Check your links: As other stories from this book have demonstrated, a failure to check your links can lead to an incredible degree of embarrassment. This story takes that lesson one step further: not only do you need to check your links to make sure they go where you think they are going, but you must review any website that you link to and make sure there is no objectionable content. Tweeting out a link makes it appear as if you endorse the content in that link. As such, always double check what you are sending.

Chapter Forty-six:

Maine Senate candidate calls openly gay Congressman "homo"

The Background: In 2014, moderate Maine Senator Susan Collins sought reelection. Collins originally had one primary opponent: Erick Bennett, a political consultant and founder of the Maine Equal Rights Center, an organization that provides "comprehensive campaign services to raise awareness regarding the impact of social issues on the loss of our Constitutional rights and liberties."

Bennett himself is no stranger to controversy. Following the death of Nelson Mandela, Bennett took to Facebook to call the beloved leader a communist terrorist:

> Nelson Mandela was no Dr. Martin Luther King and to celebrate the life of a communist terrorist who should have spent his life in prison for killing untold women and children in an attempt to create a communist state will indoctrinate a new generation in this country to follow his example. Expect to see violent

crime and poverty in the black community to continue to rise as they blindly promoted the very form of government that will enslave them. Why don't we celebrate Karl Marx and Joseph Stalin. They are literally the same thing.

Also in Maine is Congressman Michael Michaud (D-ME). In August 2013, Michaud announced that he was running for governor against the Republican incumbent, Paul LePage. In a November 2013 op-ed, Michaud confirmed a long-circulating rumor and said that he was gay.

The Fail: In a Facebook post on December 11, 2013, Bennett called Maichud a "homo" while linking him, Collins and other Maine politicians to gun confiscation efforts:

This could easily happen in Maine. Chellie Pingree, Susan Collins, Angus King and Mike Michaud are useless when it comes to protecting our rights. I know, some will say Mike Michaud would but I don't trust that guy as far as I can throw him. We are talking about a closet homo in DC who voted to discriminate against same sex couples. Not exactly what I would call a man with a conscious. We can't trust any of these people.

The Response and Consequences: Numerous Facebook commenters attacked Bennett's use of the word "homo," noting its derogatory connotations. In multiple Facebook comments, Bennett defended himself, saying that "homo" was merely short for "homosexual" while linking Democrats to slavery, for some reason:

> Homo SEXUAL, it is still a very literal term and you are ignorant of not knowing that. You can call him whatever you want. He is still a spineless coward that had the chance to take action to stop the government from oppressing people and he didnt. I have no use for someone like that.

> You dont take away peoples rights because you disagree with them. The Democrats did not want to end slavery and tried to filibuster the Republicans efforts to uphold civil rights for blacks and women but you dont see us trying to take Democrats rights away. You really think you the authority to remove a persons natural born rights because they disagree with you? You must love Hitler.

Collins and Maichud never released any statement condemning Bennett, likely fearing that such statements would only give additional oxygen to Bennett's comments. Interestingly enough, Bennett's comments were condemned by the head of the Maine Republican Party, Rick Bennett. In an interview, Rick Bennett said, "I'm happy to have a chance to discuss this because the similarities of our names have led some people say, 'Is this guy related to you?' I can say categorically he's not related to me in any way, by family or viewpoint. I find those comments personally reprehensible, and I've heard people from across the political spectrum in Maine who share their abhorrence with those views...they do not represent the views of the Republican Party." Rick Bennett also took the opportunity to say that he didn't think Erick Bennett would even make it onto the ballot, noting that it would be difficult for Erick Bennett to do so as "more people understand about his viewpoints and his character issues."

Ultimately, in March 2014, Bennett said he would leave the Republican party and run for the Senate as an Independent. However, according to Maine law, he had to leave the party by March 1, and Bennett failed to meet that deadline. As such, he did not appear on the ballot in the 2014 election.

The Lesson:

- When you are in a hole, quit digging: Bennett's initial statement was stupid enough, but he is clearly no stranger to saying outlandish things and should have known what kind of response he was going to get. The smartest thing to do would have been to never say something so ridiculous and offensive at all. The next smartest thing would have been for him to stop trying to explain and simply apologize and move on. No one actually believes that "homo" is just a word short for "homosexual." It's a word with a history of negative connotations and Bennett clearly knows this. The point is this: when you are in a hole, don't dig yourself any deeper.

Bennett managed to make himself look worse and generate even more negative bad press with his ridiculous explanation.

- Don't bring up unrelated issues: In the course of responding to criticism about his comments, Bennett started to discuss Democratic efforts to maintain slavery more than 150 years ago, resulting in a collective "Huh?" from virtually all readers. This comparison only served to make Bennett appear even crazier. When you are discussing a particular subject, don't bring up an unrelated subject that has no real relationship to the item at hand. Doing so highlights the weakness of your own defense.

Chapter Forty-seven:

The candidate who called for the hanging of President Obama

The Background: In 2014, Republican Joshua Black (@ JoshuaBlack2014) sought to unseat Democrat Dwight Dudley in Florida's 68th State House District, which is located in Pinellas County. Prior to running for the House, Black had run for President in 2012. His prior occupations included street evangelist in St. Louis. At the time of his candidacy, Black was working as a taxi driver.

The Fail: Black, like many Republicans, was highly critical of President Obama's perceived abuses of power, such as his uses of drones and prosecutions of Bradley Manning and Eric Snowden. Black, however, took things one step too far when he took to Twitter to call for the hanging of President Obama for treason:

"@civilwarcometh: @BrandonMArms
@RedNationRising I'm past impeachment. It's
time to arrest and hang him high.
Commieblaster.com" Agreed

The Response and Consequences:
Unsurprisingly, the condemnation of Black's remarks
was swift. State Representative Dwight Dudley, whom
Black was trying to unseat, said, "It's dangerous and
unbecoming for someone who wants to lead to call for
such violence and extremist action. Wow. I'm
stunned." Michael Guju, Republican Chairman of
Pinellas County, also attacked Black, saying, "It is
impossible to accept this statement. This is wholly
unacceptable and unduly pejorative."

Florida Governor Rick Scott (@FLGovScott), a
Republican, took to Twitter calling Black's remarks
outrageous and asked for his withdrawal from the
race:

> Joshua Black's comments on President @
> BarackObama are outrageous. (1/2)

> Floridians expect more from our leaders & he
> should immediately withdraw his candidacy to
> represent families of Pinellas County. (2/2)

Unsurprisingly, Black chose not to apologize for his
remarks, and issued a further explanation on
Facebook, in which he reiterated his call for Obama's
hanging:

> To everyone who was offended that I said that
> the POTUS should be hanged for treason, this is
> the man who droned Al-Awaki on "suspicion of
> terrorism"--not proof--and later killed his 15-
> year-old son for nothing more than being his
> son.

This is also the man who sought to have Bradley Manning and Eric Snowden executed for treason when they didn't kill anyone, nor does the US government pretend to believe that they cost any spies their lives.

This would be exactly what the President has done to others, and, as Jesus said, "the measure ye mete, it shall be meted to you again." I make no apologies for saying that the President is not above the People. If ordinary Americans should be executed for treason, so should he.

So, don't stop at impeachment. Remove him. Try him before a jury (the very right that he arbitrarily denied to al-Awaki and his 15-year-old son), and, upon his sure convictions, execute him. Thus has he done, thus it should be done to him.

#BenedictArnold

Perhaps the most hilarious response came from Chris Latvala (@ChrisLatvala), a fellow Republican who was running for the State House in the neighboring 67th District. Latvala forcefully engaged Black on Twitter, leading to this hilarious exchange and the creation of the hashtag #TinFoilHat:

@ChrisLatvala: @JoshuaBlack2014 you aren't serious calling for the killing of Obama are you? I know you are crazy but good heavens.U R an embarrassment

@JoshuaBlack2014: @ChrisLatvala Don't you have a race? Don't you have a primary? #MindYourOwnBusiness?

@ChrisLatvala: I make it my business when so called GOP candidates become an embarrassment to my beloved party.

@JoshuaBlack2014: Like when they sponsor legislation that funnels money to their friends or people who do business w/them? #criminalpoliticians

@ChrisLatvala: You need to go take your medicine. #TinFoilHat #Crazy #TheSecretServiceWillBeKnocking

The last of Latvala's hashtags turned out to be completely accurate: the Secret Service did visit Black for his threats. Black said that his comments were not threats but responses to the President's use of drones. Unsurprisingly, Black was crushed in the August 2014 primary, losing 80-20 percent to Bill Young II.

The Lesson:

- Call the crazy person out: Latvala won praise and press in an otherwise low profile contest by attacking Black for his nutty remarks. It's sad that the current political environment is so toxic that condemning someone when they call for the hanging of the president is considered newsworthy, it is, unfortunately, still the case. As such, don't hesitate to call out the more extreme, insane elements of politics, even when they are in your own party. After all, no matter how conservative a person is, it's doubtful that they would support a call for the execution of the president

Chapter Forty-eight:

The NBA is full of criminals, right?

The Background: Minnesota State Representative Pat Garofalo (R-58B) was first elected in 2004. Garofalo is an active Twitter user with over 3,700 followers. No stranger to controversy, Garofalo had previously made the news for a variety of less than favorable reasons, including:

- While fighting with liberal blogger Eric Pusey, Garofalo said, "Your last name tells me all I need to know about you."

- Calling a teachers' union a hate group.

- Forgetting how many women served on the Minnesota Supreme Court.

The Fail: On March 9, 2014, with no apparent provocation, Garofalo tweeted:

Let's be honest, 70% of teams in NBA could fold tomorrow + nobody would notice a difference w/possible exception of increase in streetcrime

The Response and Consequences: As of 2013, more than 75 percent of NBA players were African-American. This fact, combined with his use of "streetcrime" (as opposed to just regular crime), led many to call Garofalo and his tweet racist.

Numerous users chimed in to comment on the offensiveness of the tweet:

@PaulaC222: @PatGarofalo I'm from Minnesota and am outraged that this racist comment came from one of our representatives.

@MsMollyMpls: @PatGarofalo the total lack of respect on the first tweet and then the lack of explanation or apology on the backlash is astounding.

In an e-mail to Deadspin sent the same day of the tweet, Garofalo said, "I was talking about the NBA's high arrest rate and that their punishment for positive drug tests are weaker than other leagues. No intent beyond that."

However, the racial implications of Garofalo's tweet were clear to everyone, and Garofalo did apologize the next day. In a statement to the media (that Garofalo also tweeted), the Representative said, "In the last 24 hours, I've had the opportunity to relearn one of life's lessons: Whenever any of us are offering opinions, it is best to refer to people as individuals, as opposed to groups. Last night, I publicly commented on the NBA and I sincerely apologize to those who I unfairly categorized." Later the same day, Garofalo went in front of television cameras and said, "I take back my entire tweet. I completely apologize. It's not my intent. It's not what I believe, but I should be held accountable for my words." Garofalo also apologized, in private, to the entire Minnesota Republican House caucus.

Even more embarrassing is that Garofalo sent out the tweet because he wrongly believed that the NBA did not test for marijuana. As he had to admit later, that was completely incorrect. In the aftermath of the errand tweet, the NBA sent out their drug testing policy, which noted that players can be subjected to six random drug tests a year. Those who were found guilty were subjected to fines and penalties, including dismissal from the NBA.

The Lesson:

- Never assume a tweet will be interpreted innocently: There is no way to miss the racial implications of Garofalo's tweet. He should have been smart enough to realize that making such a broad statement against a largely African-American group would have been interpreted as racist, even if that wasn't truly his intent. In politics, you always have to assume that your tweets will be cast in the most negative light possible. Operating under that assumption can help prevent you from sending out potentially scandalous social media updates.

- Check your facts: As if the tweet itself wasn't embarrassing enough, Garofalo was incorrect. The NBA does have a drug testing policy and does deal with offenders by suspending or expelling them.

- Apologize quickly: Garofalo made a classic social media blunder. At first, he tried to explain the tweet. Less than a day later, he was apologizing, repeatedly. He should have just apologized from the start and moved on – it would have killed the story much quicker.

Chapter Forty-nine:

The $8 Billion Abortionplex and the Congressman who fell for it

The Background: The Onion is a satirical newspaper. Founded in 1988, the website (and its former print edition) mocks all aspects of society, but with a special emphasis on politics. Related to this story is Congressman John Fleming (R-LA) of Louisana's 4th Congressional District. Fleming was first elected in 2008 and established himself as a staunch conservative on all issues, including abortion: According to the National Right to Life Federation, Fleming had a perfect lifetime score on pro-life issues.

The Fail: On May 18, 2011, The Onion published an article entitled, "Planned Parenthood Opens $8 Billion Abortionplex." The article stated that the new Abortionplex would allow Planned Parenthood to "terminate unborn lives with an efficiency never before thought possible" and quoted Planned Parenthood President, Cecile Richards, as saying that abortion was the organization's "true passion."

Richards was also quoted as saying, "And since Congress voted to retain our funding, it' going to be that much easier for us to maximize the number of tiny, beating hearts we stop every day."

The article was intentionally absurd and directed at those who believe Planned Parenthood does nothing but abortion. This is not a true statement; the article itself even noted that 97 percent of Planned Parenthood's services are not related to abortion.

Less than a year later, on February 6, 2012, The Onion reran the story in response to a controversy started when the Susan B. Komen Foundation announced that they would stop funding Planned Parenthood. At this point, Congressman Fleming (or a staffer) posted the article to his Facebook page, adding, "More Planned Parenthood, abortion by the wholesale" to the link.

The Response and Consequences: The first person who commented on the post pretty much surmised what most people were thinking when they saw that Congressman Fleming had fallen for the story: "The Onion is satire. How exactly did you get elected?" The post and comment was captured in a screenshot before it was deleted.

Congressman Fleming's post was first publicized by Hudson Hongo, a blogger who runs the website Literally Unbelievable. That site is dedicated towards capturing posts made by individuals who confuse Onion stories for real news. Hongo said that a reader captured the screenshot of Fleming's error before it could be deleted and sent it to Literally Unbelievable. Said Hongo, "It seems that Rep. Fleming, like many others, has given the nearly year-old article a second life...[I find it] extremely satisfying to see a politician being made the rube by just the kind of sensationalism that they seem so adept at manufacturing these days."

The Onion was also quick to pounce on Fleming's error. Joe Randazzo, editor of The Onion, said in a statement, "We're delighted to hear that Rep. Fleming is a regular reader of America's Finest News Source and doesn't bother himself with *The New York Times*, *Washington Post*, the mediums of television and radio, or any other lesser journalism outlets."

Despite the national press that the story garnered, Congressman Fleming never commented on the post.

The Lesson:

- If it seems too bizarre to be true, make sure it's actually true: Congressman Fleming is hardly the first person to think an Onion article was true; indeed, media in China has that this issue multiple times. *The People's Daily*, the official newspaper of China, once reported on a satirical article which stated that *People Magazine* had named Kim Jong-Un the Sexiest Man Alive. In 2002, the *Beijing News* falsely reported that the U.S. Government wanted a new capitol building or it would leave the city; this story also emanated from an Onion article. However, after reading the story (completely with bizarre, over-the-top quotes), most people would quickly conclude that it was too insane to be real. Congressman Fleming (or the appropriate staffer) should have googled the story before publishing it to his Facebook page.

- Say something: If Congressman Fleming had said anything it would have been better than doing nothing. By not putting out a statement, Congressman Fleming denied himself the opportunity to put a stamp on the story, or at least rally his supporters to go after Planned Parenthood. There are any number of things he could have said: it was a staffer making posts on his behalf, it seemed like it would be true, etc. Instead, Congressman Fleming chose to keep quiet, allowing the story to develop without any input from his office.

SECTION V

Brands and Politics

Frequently a terrible, terrible mix

Anytime a business or brand gets involved in politics, it's a double-edged sword. On one hand, it gives the business a chance to express their own beliefs and curry favor among those who agree with them. However, it also can encourage backlash among opponents and ultimately be very expensive. Most of the time, businesses stay out of public advocacy. Sometimes, however, they step into politics in the worst imaginable way. Here are some examples of what happens when a business accidentally uses social media to enter the political arena.

Chapter Fifty:

Obamas gma

The Background: On October 3, 2012, the first of three presidential debates were held in Denver, Colorado. The debate featured President Barack Obama against Republican nominee Mitt Romney. Related to this fail is the US home appliance brand KitchenAid (@KitchenAid), which is owned by the Whirlpool Corporation. As the name implies, KitchenAid makes a variety of home appliances.

The Fail: At one point in the debate, while discussing Medicare and Social Security, President Obama mentioned his grandmother. KitchenAid's Twitter account then entered the realm of presidential politics with this:

> Obamas gma even knew it was going 2 b bad!
> 'She died 3 days b4 he became president'.
> #nbcpolitics

There are many, many things wrong with this tweet:

1) It's insanely insensitive.

2) It's not even remotely close to grammatically correct.

3) Obama's grandmother died one day before he was elected president, not three days before he became president.

4) It was sent by a company that makes mixers...?

The Response and Consequences: The tweet was deleted, but obviously not quickly enough. The condemnation was quick. At the peak of the disaster, which was within an hour of the original tweet, KitchenAid was getting over 1,800 mentions in a ten-minute period, eventually totaling well over 15,000. National press also covered the tweet, including *USA Today*, NBC News and the Huffington Post.

KitchenAid then proceeded to run a clinic in how to respond to a social media disaster. The first response tweet occurred eight minutes after the initial tweet was sent:

Deepest apologies for an irresponsible tweet that is in no way a representation of the brand's opinion.

A more detailed apology followed less than two and a half hours later in a series of tweets from Cynthia Soledad, the senior director of branding for KitchenAid, who tweeted under the KitchenAid account:

Hello, everyone. My name is Cynthia Soledad, and I am the head of the KitchenAid brand.

I would like to personally apologize to President @BarackObama, his family and everyone on Twitter for the offensive tweet sent earlier.

It was carelessly sent in error by a member of our Twitter team who, needless to say, won't be tweeting for us anymore.

That said, I take full responsibility for my team. Thank you for hearing me out.

Soledad made a similar statement in emails to the media.

Here's the incredible thing: KitchenAid actually gained Twitter followers from the incident, jumping from slightly over 24,000 to 26,140 within a day – an increase of more than ten percent. And if there was an impact on sales, it wasn't felt by Whirlpool, KitchenAid's parent company, which reported beating its earnings estimates for the next two quarters after the errand tweet.

The Lesson:

- Take personal responsibility: As you can see in Soledad's statement, the head of the department took personal responsibility for the error made. She offered a personal apology, noted who was to blame but took the heat herself. Taking responsibility is exactly what someone should do in an apology. It makes it more personal and authentic.

- Speed in two parts: Kitchen Aid deserves credit for its very quick response. The first apology went out in eight minutes, and the second in less than three hours. The brand recognized the severity of their mistake and quickly responded. More to the point, they responded in two parts: an immediate, no frills apologize and a more detailed one a few hours later. This shows that you can, in fact, send out multiple (though coordinated) messages. Sometimes, it's better to be fast than perfect, as long as the "perfect" apology is forthcoming.

Chapter Fifty-one:

Don't confuse a dress with a mass shooting

The Background: This is the second social media scandal that erupted as a result of the Aurora Theater shootings. On July 20, James Holmes opened fire on a sold-out midnight premier of "The Dark Knight Rises," killing 12 and injuring 70. Naturally, in the wake of the shooting, topics related to the massacre began to trend on Twitter. This included the word "Aurora." Unrelated until this day was the online retailer CelebBoutique.com (@CelebBoutique). Based in Britain, the website sells women's clothing and accessories. One of those dresses was the Aurora, a dress which was inspired by Kim Kardashian and could give buyers her "goddess worthy look" for a mere $159.75.

The Fail: This astoundingly insensitive tweet was sent a mere hour after the shooting:

> #Aurora is trending, clearly about our Kim K inspired #Aurora dress;) Shop: celebboutique.com/aurora-white-p...

The Response and Consequences: After being left up for over an hour, Celeb Boutique deleted the tweet and sent out this response:

> We are incredibly sorry for our tweet about Aurora – Our PR is NOT US based and had not checked the reason for the trend, at that time our
>
> social media was totally UNAWARE of the situation and simply thought it was another trending topic – we have removed the very insensitive
>
> tweet and will of course take more care in future to look into what we say in our tweets. Again we do apologise for any offense caused
>
> this was not intentional & will not occur again. Our most sincere apologies for both the tweet and situation. - CB

Of course this was not enough to stem the furor over the tweet. By the end of the day, thousands of people joined a Facebook group that called for a boycott of Celeb Boutique. The hacker group Anonymous (@YourAnonNews) then got in on the act, threatening to take down Celeb Boutique's website:

> Dear Internet: Let's shut these insensitive fuckers down >> @celebboutique (see:bit.ly/Q9VUmmF)

At least one reporter at Mashable would go as far as to say that Celeb Boutique sent the tweet on purpose, seizing on the wink emoticon at the end of the tweet as evidence that they knew exactly what they were doing. The article noted that Celeb Boutique had sent over 15,000 tweets and had over 43,000 followers at the time they sent the tweet. They weren't new to Twitter and should have known better. This is a bit hard to believe. No company would intentionally make such a foolish decision knowing what negative press it would generate.

The Lesson:

- Look before you leap: This was likely an honest mistake. Had the person tweeting realized why "Aurora" was trending, there is no way they ever would have sent out this tweet. However, common sense should have stopped the tweet from being sent out in the first place. If something is trending related to your brand but you don't know why, it's worth it to check out the reason for the trend before the tweet. Furthermore, it's always worth it to quickly glance at your twitter stream before sending out a tweet, in order to make sure that no major events are happening locally or world-wide that would make your tweet appear insensitive.

- If you outsource, do so smartly: The fact that Celeb Boutique's public relations firm was not located in the United States provides a lesson in outsourcing for politicians and anyone who uses social media. If you are going to outsource, do so smartly. Sometimes, mistakes can't be helped. That being said, they are certainly compounded when the company that you use for outsourcing is incompetent. A basic tenant of twitter is to check what people are tweeting about before you join in on a conversation. This PR company failed. For politicians, the lesson is simpler: If you are going to outsource social media, make sure you do so to someone who understands the basic tenants of politics and the internet.

- Put your money where your mouth is when your foot is in your mouth: Many articles about the subject called for Celeb Boutique to make a donation to an Aurora-related fund in the aftermath of this snafu. That would have been smart and showed genuine contrition; doing so with the proceeds for any Aurora dresses would have been even smarter. That never happened, and this was a missed opportunity.

Chapter Fifty-two:

Don't confuse clothing with a revolution

The Background: In February 2011, Egypt was burning. Triggered by corruption, electoral fraud and police brutality, the country was undergoing a revolution in an effort to topple the regime of Hosni Mubarak, ruler of Egypt. The revolution was ultimately successful in that goal but not without a price: Over 850 were killed and thousands more were injured. As of February 3, hundreds of thousands were protesting across the country. President Mubarak was refusing to step down and supporters of Mubarak were riding through Tahrir Square in Cairo, complete with wooden sticks that they were using to beat protestors.

As has since become standard for events like this, Twitter's trending topics section reflected the revolution that was garnering world-wide attention. #Cairo was one of those trending topics.

The Fail: This astoundingly insensitive tweet, sent out on February 3, 2011, from designer Kenneth Cole's (@ KennethCole) personal account:

Millions are in uproar in #Cairo. Rumor is they heard our new spring collection is available online at http://bit.ly/KCairo - KC

The link itself pointed to Cole's spring collection. The "KC" signature at the end of the tweet indicated that the tweet had been sent directly from Cole himself, not a staffer.

The Response and Consequences: This lasted five hours before it was deleted. Two subsequent tweets from Cole followed:

Re Egypt tweet: we weren't intending to make light of a serious situation. We understand the sensitivity of this historic moment.

I have removed this morning's tweet. Please visit this link to see my apology. http://on.fb.me/fCSf5Z - KC

That tweet lead to this longer apology on Facebook:

I apologize to everyone who was offended by my insensitive tweet about the situation in Egypt. I've dedicated my life to raising awareness about serious social issues, and in hindsight my attempt at humor regarding a nation liberating themselves against oppression was poorly timed and absolutely inappropriate.

Kenneth Cole, Chairman and Chief Creative Officer

Among the responses was a classic parody account, @ KennethColePR:

Jeffrey Dahmer would have eaten up our spring collection! #KennethColeTweets

Astoundingly, as a marketing ploy, the tweet worked. The link Cole tweeted out, which lead to Cole's website, was clicked on more than 15,000 times. In a September 2013 interview with *Boots Magazine*, Cole himself confirmed that bad tweets were good business. "Billions of people read my inappropriate, self-promoting tweet, I got a lot of harsh responses, and we hired a crisis management firm...But our stock went up that day, our e-commerce business was better, the business at every one of our stores improved, and I picked up 3,000 new followers on Twitter. So on what criteria is this a gaffe?"

And no, Cole wasn't even slightly apologetic. "Within hours, I tweeted an explanation, which had to be vetted by lawyers," he added. "I'm not even sure I used the words I'm sorry -- because I wasn't sorry."

This line of questioning came up in his interview because in September 2013, Cole used political events to sell merchandise again (though at least this time, he had the decency to not include a link). At the time, an international crisis was exploding in Syria and a world-wide debate was underway as to what sort of response the international community should make. The phrase "boots on the ground" was being used frequently by President Obama and Secretary of State Kerry. Cole's tweet:

"Boots on the ground" or not, let's not forget about sandals, pumps and loafers. #Footwear

The Lesson:

- Don't use violent current events to sell your merchandise, or yourself: No matter what your line of work is, using violence, war and government suppression to sell your product is probably a bad business strategy. Sure, you may get a boost of attention, but at what price? There is more leeway for politicians here, since elected officials naturally deal with controversial issues to make broader points about public policy. However, being too overt about using tragedy for political gain can be damaging. Case in point: the dispute that former President George W. Bush engendered when he used images of 9/11 in political ads. More recently was the case of Congressman Tim Griffin (R-AR). When a shooting occurred on Capitol Hill in October 2013, Griffin angrily took to Twitter and used the unfolding tragedy to attack Democrats. "Stop the violent rhetoric President Obama, Chuck Schumer and Nancy Pelosi. #disgusting" The tweet was even more offensive because the shooting was literally unfolding as Griffin was tweeting and the entire incident turned out to be related to a mentally ill woman who tried to crash the White House gates with her car. Griffin did apologize and delete the tweet. The point is this: some things shouldn't be touched in marketing, or in politics.

- Or, use controversy to sell your merchandise... if it fits your image... and you have the stomach for it: Cole proved that tactless tweets, depending on who and what, can be good business. As Cole himself admitted, this company had frequently used controversy to sell. In 2011, shortly after the Egypt tweet, Cole launched a website intended to stir debates on various controversy subjects like gun control and gay marriage. Of course, half of the website was used to sell shoes. In an Instagram video, Cole said he made comments like this in an effort to "start a conversation" and "promote dialogue about important issues." Naturally, in the process, Cole sells more shoes. So what's the takeaway? If it fits into your image, controversy can sell. That being said, at the end of the day, you have to sleep at night, and I'm really not sure how Cole does it.

SECTION VI

Whoops

Ridiculous mistakes

Technical mistakes happen to the savviest social media user. Unfortunately for the victims of these errors, the slightest mistake can have the most disastrous of consequences. Missing one button or a typo of just one letter can turn an innocuous tweet into a national news story. Small, technical errors are to blame for some of the more catastrophic tweets involving government and politicians. Below are some of the finer examples.

ঙ০ ০৪

Chapter Fifty-three:

They dislike you; they really, really dislike you

The Background: In 2012, Texas Governor Rick Perry sought the Republican nomination for president. After initially rocketing to the top of the polls, Perry stumbled after repeated mistakes, including a nationally televised debate in which he said that he defended his policy of giving in-state tuition rates to the children of illegal immigrants and attacked opponents by saying he didn't think they "had a heart."

The Fail: With his conservative credentials under attack, Perry was forced to leap to the right on social issues. As a result, Perry cut a 30-second ad for a video called "Strong" that appeared on YouTube and in Iowa. The topic of the video was a conservative favorite: gays and Obama's "war on religion." The video premiered on December 7, 2011, and featured Perry outdoors, talking directly into the camera:

"I'm not ashamed to admit that I'm a Christian. But you don't need to be in the pew every Sunday to know that there's something wrong with this country when gays can serve openly in the military but our kids can't openly celebrate Christmas or pray in school. As president, I'll end Obama's War on Religion and I'll fight against liberal attacks on our religious heritage. Faith made America strong; it can make her strong again. I'm Rick Perry, and I approve this message."

The Response and Consequences: The video was, far and away, the most viewed on Perry's YouTube channel, with over 8,850,000 views as of March 2014. Aware of how much controversy the video would generate, Perry's campaign disabled comments on the video. However, they forgot to disable another critical feature: the like and dislike buttons. YouTube viewers can "like" or "dislike" a video by clicking a button. The results are instantly tabulated and made publicly available. And Perry's campaign neglected to disable that feature.

Over 300,000 people disliked the video within two days, making it one of the most disliked videos ever to appear on YouTube, surpassing Rebecca Black's "Friday." Even more incredible was that the video had only been viewed 750,000 times at this point, but had still managed to amass 300,000 dislikes, meaning that an astounding 40 percent of all viewers had disliked the video.

Oops.

The Perry campaign eventually disabled commenting and likes on every one of their videos, thereby deleting one of the primary benefits of social media: the ability of people to give feedback. Of course, at this point the damage had been done. Over 500,000 people had clicked on the dislike button by the time the feature was disabled. The story on the dislikes also appeared in a variety of national media outlets, including the Huffington Post, Mashable and *Time Magazine*. For a politician who was trying to prove his competency and electability, it didn't get much worse than this. Of course, the video was also ripe for parodies, of which there is no shortage: a YouTube search for "Rick Perry Strong Parody" yields over 14,000 results.

This was just the latest in a series of errors for Perry. In previous debates, he compared Social Security to a Ponzi scheme. He infamously forgot the name of the three federal departments that he wanted to cut. Perry then failed to qualify for the Virginia ballot, confused the voting age and 2012 election date (in one sentence), and gave multiple bizarre speeches that had pundits openly wondering if he was on drugs. Perry epitomized the phrase "not ready for prime time" and dropped out of the presidential race after a disappointing fifth place Iowa finish.

The Lesson:

- Know all of your media: Clearly, someone in Perry's campaign forgot to do their research. Disabling the like/dislike feature on a YouTube video is a matter of clicking one button. The Perry campaign missed this simple step and paid a price for it. The lesson for politicians is to make sure that you (or your team) understand all of the technical aspects of social media.

- Be ready for backlash: The overwhelmingly negative response that "Strong" received should have been indicative of just how bad the video was. Indeed, many reports noted that there was intense division within the Perry campaign on the language used in the video. The campaign should have expected this and been ready to respond. Indeed, given Perry's language in the ad and clear strategy to mobilize evangelicals to his side, it would have made perfect tactical sense for Perry to say that the intense response of the video was from liberals and Obama supporters who wanted to derail his campaign because they were afraid of him. Such a statement could have helped Perry further mobilize his base. However, there was no response from the Perry campaign, except to quietly disable many of the social aspects of their social media outlets. The campaign should have seen this coming and been better prepared for it.

Chapter Fifty-four:

Missile Inbound! Run and Hide! J/K

The Background: With 3.7 million people living within its borders, Yokohama is the largest incorporated city in Japan. The city itself is located a mere 800 miles from North Korea, which is well within the range of North Korean missiles. Given the state of relations between North Korea and the rest of the civilized world, Yokohama is understandably on alert for military action from its neighbor and has numerous emergency plans in place in the event that North Korea does launch an attack. Some of those plans involve the utilization of social media. April 2013 was a particularly tense time for the city, as that was when North Korea was expected to test its mid-range missiles.

The Fail: On April 10, 2013, the City of Yokohama sent out a tweet from their official account, which stated: "North Korea has launched a missile" with blank spaces left to indicate the time of the supposed missile launch.

The Response and Consequences: The tweet was up for 20 minutes before being deleted and replaced by an apology from Yokohama. The city acknowledged that no missile had been launched and the tweet was sent out accidentally. It was only deleted when they received a phone call from a follower who noticed the tweet and became concerned. In the apology, Yokohama said that the tweet had been created in advance as part of an emergency management plan. However, the "mechanism" that would have sent the tweet failed and the tweet was launched early and incorrectly.

The Lesson:

- Planning is good: Rather than concentrate completely on the fail, it's important to note that Yokohama had appropriately incorporated social media into an emergency action plan. This is vital and necessary in today's society. As a report from the United States Department of Homeland Security noted after Hurricane Sandy, "Social media and collaborative technologies have become critical components of emergency preparedness, response and recovery." Indeed, it behooves all levels of government to incorporate social media with any such emergency plan.

- Execution is better: Assuming that this tweet was sent by a program like Hootsuite, it was probably a matter of someone clicking the "send" button, instead of the "save" one. This story serves as a reminder for all social media users to make sure they double check before clicking anything on Twitter, including what account they are tweeting from and whether or not they are saving a tweet to be sent later or scheduling one to be sent now.

Chapter Fifty-five:

Holy Pope, Batman!

The Background: Twitter has come such a long way that it has been embraced by one of the most traditional institutions in the world: the Vatican. Starting in December 2012, Pope Benedict XVI started a Twitter account. When Benedict XVI resigned as pope, all tweets were completely deleted, only to be replaced by Pope Francis' likeliness upon his ascension to the Papacy. The account regularly tweets Catholic doctrine, prayers and invocations. Of course, this is not the only Vatican-related Twitter account. There are dozens of others; one of those is Vatican Communications, which tweets as @PCCS_VA.

The Fail: This random tweet:

Holy switcheroo! Bathman has grown bitter, more vengeful with the years bit.ly/11nYyul

The link itself took readers to a story that was actually posted on a Vatican news website, the Pontifical Council for Social Communications. The story itself dealt with the evolving nature of Batman in the movies. The pope and Catholic Church were never mentioned.

The Response and Consequences: The original concern, including by the AP, was that the Vatican account had been hacked. Indeed, Monsignor Paul Tighe, the second-in-command of the Vatican's Communication Office, originally thought that was the case. However, upon further investigation, the Vatican eliminated those concerns, saying that they had run the tweet accidentally. The Vatican blamed the tweet on an "internal system failure" and said that a non-native English speaker had misunderstood the Batman story.

One thing that can be said here: it isn't often that E! Online runs a story about the Vatican, but this tweet put the pope on E!. It's also worth noting that the tweet and story were never deleted. It remains visible on Twitter and on the PCSC's website.

The Lesson:

- Make sure you speak the language well: This might be obvious, but make sure that, if someone is tweeting on your behalf, they have a full understanding of your language. This will prevent inappropriate content from being be created and tweeted, as well as avoiding situations in which even more inappropriate content can be responded to or retweeted.

- Have a thorough review system in place: Even if this post was due to a mere English misunderstanding, the Vatican should have had a better review system in place to ensure that inappropriate content wasn't tweeted out to begin with. Some kind of double check could have saved them this embarrassment. For personal twitter accounts, this type of system may not be possible as speed is of the essence. However, for an account like Vatican Communications, taking an extra five minutes to double check content wouldn't be a massive impediment.

Chapter Fifty-six:

Constituent service

The Background: Rob Wilson (@RobWilson_RDG) is a member of Great Britain's Parliament and has served the people of Reading East since 2005. In that capacity, he served a variety of positions, including Shadow Higher Education Minister and Parliamentary Private Secretary for the Secretary of State for Culture. Like many Members of Parliament, Wilson has a relatively active Twitter account that had over 7,000 followers as of January 2015.

The Fail: This innocuous tweet:

I see Guido has a piece about the #BBC's interview with IDS. A formal complaint to Lord Hall. Deserved in this case. Tinyurl.com/cp2nso

The tweet in question referred to a story that was posted on the Guido Fawkes political blog, in which Tory MP Dominic Raab complained to the BBC Director General about a story they had run that attacked Work and Pensions Secretary Duncan Smith. All normal political stuff. The problem? The tweet actually went to Sexydigg.com. That site featured girls in bikinis and links to hardcore porn and live sex shows.

The Response and Consequences: The tweet was deleted in 14 minutes by an aide. Numerous reports indicated that Wilson was very angry over the error, which was apparently not his fault, as Wilson didn't create the link himself. Rather, it was sent to him via Conservative Party headquarters. According to a source at the Conservative Party, "Rob Wilson expressed an interest in a story and he was sent a link. It appears there was a technical glitch and we are looking into it." In other words, Wilson was not to blame, according to his own party. The link ending in "cp2nso" went to Sexydigg, but a link ending with "cp25nso" went to the article. In other words, a missing "5" was responsible for this blooper.

The Lesson:

- Look before you link: No matter the source, always check a link before tweeting it out. Short links like the one Wilson used have no way of indicating where they will take you until you click on them, a lesson that Wilson learned the hard way.

Chapter Fifty-seven:

An unexpected endorsement

The Background: Meg Whitman is a highly successful American business executive. She worked for a variety of successful businesses, including Walt Disney, DreamWorks, Hasbro and Proctor & Gamble. From 1998-2008, she served as president and CEO of eBay, where she oversaw tremendous growth of the company, albeit not without significant controversy. In 2010, she sought to parlay her business success into the political arena when she ran as the Republican nominee for governor of California. 2010 was a fantastic year for Republicans and Whitman was thought to have a real chance at capturing the governor's office. During the campaign, Whitman's staff included Sarah Pompei (@sarahpompei), a spokeswoman for the campaign.

The Fail: In October 2010, Whitman was endorsed by the San Diego Deputy Sheriff's Association. Using her personal account, Pompei sent out the following tweet:

> SD Cnty Sheriff Assoc says @Whitman2010 4 gov! RT: @Murphy4MegNews CA Cops get it: Jerry Brown is too soft on crime. http://bit.ly/bNCAV

All pretty standard stuff, with one problem: the link did not follow to the endorsement. An "r" was missing from the short link. Instead, the tweet went to a YouTube video featuring H.J. Freaks, a bass playing, Korean cross-dresser.

The Response and Consequences: "For the record, no word on whether the cross-dressing bassist has endorsed anyone for Governor," quipped California's ABC13 news. Naturally, the tweet went viral and appeared on numerous national websites and blogs (as a general rule, if you are a candidate for office and something your staff does appears on Gawker, it's a bad thing).

So, you'd think this tweet was deleted almost immediately, right? Wrong. Pompei left this tweet up for an astounding two days before deleting. "How smart is it of Pompei, or Team Whitman, to allow the tweet to remain on the spokeswoman's Twitter stream?" wondered the *Los Angeles Times*, which is the most widely read paper in California.

When asked to comment about the bad link, Pompei responded with one word: "Oopsie."

The tweet itself was symbolic of Whitman's struggling campaign. At the time of the goof, which occurred barely three weeks before the general election, polls showed Brown ahead of Whitman by nine points. Whitman would ultimately spend more than $140 million of her own money on the losing effort.

The Lesson:

- Correct your tweets: No matter how careful you are, bad tweets happen. It's human nature to make mistakes. That being said, correct your errors as soon as possible. For whatever reason, Pompei left this tweet up for two days before deleting it. This is a lifetime in Twitter-time and an inexcusable mistake that simply helped to fuel the story along. When you make a mistake, correct it ASAP, take responsibility for it, and move on. Don't let it just sit there.

Chapter Fifty-eight:

You spelled "bigger" wrong

The Background: Since the start of the Obama administration, Dan Pfeiffer (@pfeiffer44) has worked for the White House. During the president's first term, he served as Director of Communications. In Obama's second term, he switched positions to become the Senior Adviser to the President for Strategy and Communications. Like many in the Obama administration, Pfeiffer is an active user on Twitter.

The Fail: On October 8, 2013, Pfeiffer was having a Twitter exchange with *New York Times* reporter Jonathan Martin on an NBC First Read article that described how the rise of the internet and cable TV were contributing factors to increased political polarization in America. Unfortunately for Pfeiffer, the conversation went completely awry with one typo:

> @jmartNYT also a much nigger factor on the right

The Response and Consequences: Pfeiffer realized his mistake, deleted his original tweet and uploaded an apology within four minutes:

Obviously a horrendous typo in my previous tweet. My apologies

In all fairness, this particular typo wasn't the craziest one – on a standard QWERTY keyboard, the "b" and "n" are next to each other. Fortunately for Pfeiffer, while the typo made some brief waves and earned him some scorn among Obama detractors, it quickly faded away. Pfeiffer continued to work for the Obama White House.

The Lesson:

- Typos matter, so check your tweets: If you need any proof about just how badly you can damage yourself and your career with a single letter, this is it. Sure, this was a total accident and Pfeiffer emerged unscathed, but can you imagine the terror that Pfeiffer must have felt when he first sent out this tweet? Or the conversation he had with President Obama? "Umm, Mr. President, hi...I accidentally tweeted the n-word. Yes, accidentally...." All of this could have been avoided if Pfeiffer had just checked his tweet before sending it.

Chapter Fifty-nine:

"Piece" of mind

The Background: In the run-up to the deadline to buy health insurance on HealthCare.Gov, President Obama and the White House (@WhiteHouse) took to social media to promote people buying health insurance. Using the hashtag #GetCovered, the Obama administration tweeted a series of pictures that contained reasons why individuals should purchase health care insurance.

The Fail: On December 12, 2013, the White House sent out this tweet:

#GetCovered because your mom will have peace of mind (and you will as well).

HealthCare.gov

The tweet also included a picture with the same slogan. Unfortunately, the picture said that those who got health care coverage would give their mother's "piece of mind." The pic used the wrong "piece" –

what would have been grammatically appropriate was "peace."

The Response and Consequences: Since its launch on October 1, the HealthCare.Gov website had suffered from a variety of technical problems, tanking the public's confidence in the law and pushing Obama's approval ratings to record lows for his administration. The grammar blooper further pushed the idea of an incompetent White House. If they didn't know the difference between "peace" and "piece," how could they be trusted to overhaul a sector of the U.S. economy that consumed 1/6 of the nation's gross domestic product?

Conservatives jumped on the chance to mock Obama for the error. "Remember when everybody told us that Obama was the smartest President we ever had? If he's so smart, why doesn't he know the difference between Piece of Mind and Peace of Mind?" asked the conservative website Fire Andrea Mitchell. The Daily Caller appropriately labeled the grammar error a #SpellingFail. Even more Obama-friendly websites like the Huffington Post covered the goof.

Perhaps most interesting was that this tweet, unlike many that have obvious grammar or spelling issues, was never deleted. Doing so would likely have opened the Obama administration up to claims that they were trying to cover up the mistake.

Somewhat fortuitously for the Obama administration, internet attention on #GetCovered was divided. Earlier in the same day, a post appeared with Obama holding a hand-written sign about the importance of purchasing health insurance. The sign read, "Nobody should go broke just because they got sick!" However, such a sign was practically made to be photoshopped. Within hours of the tweet's initial publication, a meme started featuring a variety of messages, some related to Obama and Health Care, many not. Fake messages and pictures included:

- "Obamacare cancelled the plan that you had and liked!" That one was courtesy of Senator Ted Cruz.

- A picture labeled "Obamacare 2013," featuring a literal train wreck.

- "Welcome to Kenya!"

- "I lied."

The meme helped to distract the internet and the "piece" blooper earned less press than it would have otherwise.

The Lesson:

- Call the grammar police: While not earth-shattering, the error promoted the idea of an incompetent White House. As this mistake showed, grammar matters, particularly when you are operating at the level of the White House. A good strategy to avoid these mistakes is to have another person review tweets for grammar and spelling.

SECTION VII

With malicious intent

Tweets intentionally designed to cause havoc and wreak harm

More often than not, the stories featured in this book were accidents: The person who committed the error didn't realize what they were doing when they sent out an errant tweet or made that stupid Facebook post. At a bare minimum, they didn't think they were doing anything wrong. This section contains the exceptions to that rule: the times when a person or organization was using social media to create as much havoc as possible.

৪০ ০৪

Chapter Sixty:

The hacking of the AP

The Background: A twitter account getting hacked is nothing new. By April 2013, multiple prominent Twitter accounts had been hacked, including President Obama, Britney Spears, Justin Beiber, Lady GaGa, Jeep and Burger King, among others. Many of these accounts were hacked by the Syrian Electronic Army, a group of hackers that is affiliated with the government of Syrian President Bashar al-Assad.

The Fail: On April 23, 2013, at 1:07pm, this tweet appeared from the Associate Press (@AP) official account:

> Breaking; Two Explosions in the White House and Barack Obama is injured

The Response and Consequences: Within minutes after the tweets were sent, the Dow Jones dropped 145 points while other markets reacted similarly. $136 billion in equity was erased in two minutes. The attack helped to highlight the problem of high frequency trading (HFT), which is trading that occurs on the basis of a variety of computer algorithms and other technological tools. When computers discovered news of a possible assassination attempt on the president, they sold stocks, triggering other HFT programs to kick in and sell more stocks, creating a cascade effect. Ultimately, the markets bounced back when it became apparent that the news story was false, and the Dow and other markets went up that day.

To their credit, after the original tweet, the AP responded quickly. AP Reporter Sam Hananel (@SamHammelAP) refuted the tweet three minutes after it was originally sent:

Please Ignore AP Tweet on explosions, we've been hacked.

At 1:13pm, other AP branded tweets jumped in to deny the tweet:

@APStylebook: The @AP Twitter account has been suspended after it was hacked. The tweet about an attack on the White House was false.

@AP_Fashion: The AP Twitter account has been hacked. No reports of bombings at the White House or injuries to the president.

The scandal reached the White House, where during the afternoon briefing, White House Press Secretary Jay Carney noted that the report was obviously false and said that the president was just fine.

Within ten minutes of the AP hack, the Syrian Electronic Army (@Official_SEA6) took responsibility for the hack, complete with a link to a screenshot of the AP page:

- Ops! @AP get owned by Syrian Electronic Arm! #SEA #Syria #ByeByeObama pic.twitter.com/HTKoO6gIL6

The AP was able to get its main Twitter account suspended, along with all of its other branded accounts. The rogue tweet was deleted and it wasn't until the following day that its Twitter accounts were restored, at which point the AP tweeted:

The @AP Twitter account, which was suspended after being hacked, has been secured and is back up. Thank you for your patience. - @EricCarvin

As for how the account was actually hacked: The problem began because multiple people had access to the password for the AP's Twitter account. At the time, Twitter did not have a two-factor authentication; this process requires that a password be matched to a number that is paired with a user's cellphone, thus dramatically enhancing an account's security. Instead, the AP fell victim to a phishing scandal. Less than an hour before the tweet occurred, the SEA was able to break into an AP staffer's email account and send an email to other AP employee's. The email contained a link to a "*Washington Post* story" and a note to "read the following article, it's very important." When users went to the *Washington Post* story, it actually required that they input their Twitter username and password. That information went directly to the SEA. AP Security responded to the initial Email 17 minutes after it was sent, urging users not to click the link, but by then it was too late and the account was hacked.

The AP would write a story on the hack and its subsequent effect on the stock market, posting a story about six hours after the initial hack. The headline: "Hackers Compromise AP Twitter Account." Within a month, Twitter introduced two-step authentication.

The Lesson:

- Train your staff: Staff training is critical to recognizing and defeating any phishing attempt. It is vital that any staff that has access to your social media accounts be trained to recognize signs that a phishing email has been sent. These include generic greetings, poor grammar, websites that don't actually lead you to the page displayed in text, absence of logos and suspicious attachments. Appropriate staff training could have saved the AP a lot of grief here.

- Use all security measures: Even the best training won't get around a good phishing email. As such, make sure you use every security measure available to you. Twitter and virtually every other social network now utilizes two-step authentication. If your account is prominent, this is a must have. Among other vital security precautions: change your password frequently and limit access to your account.

- Have a plan in place: When hacked, the AP acted on either a very good communications plan or impressive improvisation. They sent out statements via press release, news wire, blogs, Twitter and Facebook from all of their branded accounts. They also asked people not to communicate with or retweet their compromised account. Then they were able to get their compromised account (and many non-compromised accounts) taken down and back up. Even if a crisis-management plan wasn't in place, they certainly did an outstanding job of communicating with everyone possible to resolve the crisis. What happened was obviously terrible. As previously noted, it erased $136 billion in two minutes, but the crisis management plan they had in place was so good that the money was almost completely restored within ten minutes of being first erased.

Chapter Sixty-one:

Malicious tweets during Hurricane Sandy

The Background: In late October 2012, Hurricane Sandy slammed into the Northeast United States. The Hurricane became the second costliest American hurricane of all time, killing 125 and causing $62 billion in damage. The storm also put more than six million Americans in the dark for days at a time. As a result, many picked up their wireless devices and turned to Twitter for their news. Naturally, this resulted in a great degree of misinformation being flung around the internet in a demonstration of what one news article called the "dark side of Social Media." This included pictures of flooding at the New York Stock Exchange, a photo of a three-foot wave hitting the Statue of Liberty and erroneous reports of the New York City's Fire Department headquarters being evacuated.

The Fail: Twitter user @comfortablysmug used Hurricane Sandy to spread malicious and intentionally false rumors on Twitter. Labeled with "BREAKING" headers, @comfortablysmug tweeted numerous pieces of misinformation. Among the fake news:

1) Con Edison was shutting down all power to Manhattan.

2) Governor Cuomo was trapped in Manhattan.

3) The New York Stock Exchange was flooded with over three feet of water.

4) The entire New York City subway system would be shut down for the remainder of the week, with all major lines flooded and in need of repair.

The Response and Consequences: As the tweets first circulated, many attempted to correct the misinformation, including Con Ed's official Twitter account, which directly refuted the claim that Manhattan's power was being shut down. Meanwhile, it took BuzzFeed a day to identify @comfortablysmug as 29-year-old Shashank Tripathi. Tripathi was a one-time hedge fund analyst who was managing the campaign of Christopher Wright, congressional candidate in New York's 12th District, at the time of the tweets. BuzzFeed called Tripathi "Hurricane Sandy's Worst Twitter Villain" and the story was quickly picked up by national media.

The same day that he was identified, Tripathi tweeted an apology:

I wish to offer the people of New York a sincere, humble and unconditional apology.

During a natural disaster that threatened the entire city, I made a series of irresponsible and inaccurate tweets.

While some would use the anonymity and instant feedback of social media as an excuse, I take full responsibility for my actions. I deeply regret any distress or harm they may have caused.

I have resigned from the congressional campaign of Christopher Wight, effective immediately. Wight is a candidate with the ideas, philosophy and leadership skills to make New York a better place and who will be an outstanding advocate for the people of the 12th Congressional District. It is my sincere hope that the voters of New York will see him based on his merits alone, and not my actions of the last 24 hours.

Again, I offer my sincere apologies.

Many, including New York City Councilman Peter Vallone, Jr., called for charges against Tripathi, comparing the tweets to yelling fire in a crowded theater.

Tripathi was fortunate that no charges were filed. Even those pushing for charges, like Vallone, acknowledged that it would be a very difficult case to make. However, as the apology noted, Tripathi was publicly vilified and forced to resign his job as a campaign manager. Incidentally, his former employer lost after earning just 19 percent of the vote in the election.

The Lesson:

- Facts matter: This should go without saying, but don't tweet things out that you know are not true.

- Don't expect anonymity: In this digital age, you leave a footprint everywhere you go. Do not expect to be anonymous and always assume that everything you say and do on social media can – and will – go public.

Chapter Sixty-two:

The anti-Obama Wonk

The Background: The National Security Council is a U.S. agency whose mission is to "lead the U.S. Government in cryptology that encompasses both Signals Intelligence (SIGINT) and Information Assurance (IA) products and services, and enables Computer Network Operations (CNO) in order to gain a decision advantage for the Nation and our allies under all circumstances." In other words, people responsible for the nation's safety and security. Clearly, all employees must go through extensive background checks that include "medical screening, a polygraph interview, drug test and extensive background investigation."

The Fail: For two years, a Twitter account named @NatSecWonk tweeted flippant, obnoxious and biting commentary that was often directed at the Obama administration and the U.S. government as a whole. Of course, there are literally thousands of parody accounts that rip into the government. However, the information tweeted "often contained insider details" that appeared to be leaked information from the White

House briefings. Although not classified, this did imply that a relatively high ranking staffer must have had access.

Among the tweets:

> I feel sorry for John Kerry's press handlers, who are cleaning up one shit storm after the other he is creating on his current Asia swing.

> Someone at #aspenideas should ask Valerie Jarrett what it is that she actually does at the White House #ihavenoideadoyou?

And that's just some of the highlights. @NatSecWonk took shots at people from across the political spectrum but saved most of his firepower for fellow Democrats, including President Obama, Secretary of State Hillary Clinton, National Security Adviser Susan Rice and U.N. Ambassador Samantha Power. He went after the physical appearance and weight of many, including Liz Cheney and Ann Romney. The tweets went so far as to question the sexual orientation of Senator Lindsey Graham (R-SC). All of this is relatively standard (albeit disgusting) behavior for anonymous trolls that tweet, but it was viewed particularly shocking since it appeared to be coming from an actual Obama administration employee.

The Response and Consequences: The Twitter account disappeared in mid-October, 2013. At that time, @NatSecWonk was identified as Jofi Joseph, 40, who served as a nonproliferation expert at the NSA.

In a statement to Politico, Joseph took full responsibility for the account. "It has been a privilege to serve in this Administration and I deeply regret violating the trust and confidence placed in me." Among Joseph's responsibilities was working with NSA staff on sensitive, classified issues, including working on the team that opened negotiations with Iran over their nuclear programs. Even worse, Joseph was suspected of also being behind another anonymous account, @dchobbyist. That account tweeted about the State Department, sexual encounters and escort services. Prior to working for the NSA, Joseph had worked at the State Department. Joseph had no comment about whether or not he was behind @dchobbyist.

It took many months of investigative work for Joseph to be caught. Indeed, White House investigators eventually tried catching Joseph by intentionally giving him inaccurate information to see if it would appear on the @NatSecWonk Twitter feed. The arrest of Joseph took many by surprise. "It was like they were hunting for Bin Laden in a cave and he was right in the belly of the beast all along," one former NSC official told the *Washington Post*. Senator Bob Casey (D-PA), for whom Joseph had once worked, said he was "stunned" at the revelation that Joseph was @NatSecWonk, noting that he "saw no sign of this kind of behavior."

The Lesson:

- Don't tweet trade secrets: You can file this one under "this really needs to be said, apparently" but never, ever tweet anything that is confidential or that you have questions about tweeting.

- There is no anonymity: Joseph clearly thought he was smart enough not to get caught, and for almost two years, that was accurate. However, in the end, it was his own words that did him in. According to a Politico article, White House lawyers tracked Joseph down after comparing his travel and shopping patterns to the over 2,000 tweets that he sent out from @ NatSecWonk. In other words, living life is exactly what got Joseph caught. Nothing put on social media is truly anonymous, and if you have read this book, you know how easy it is to be caught.

SECTION VIII

The Takeaways

Final lessons

No matter how good you are or how much you plan, mistakes will happen. You will say something stupid, a staffer will mishandle something or a disgruntled intern will hack your account. All of these things have happened; elected officials have also survived them all.

As you have likely noted, each situation is different, but there are striking similarities across most, if not all of them: poor controls and planning over a social media account, a total lack of judgment, and an unforced error compounded by an inadequate response.

Broadly speaking, there are two ways to deal with social media screw-ups: Preventing them to begin with and what to do when they occur. First, a look at the preventative measures:

Training for yourself and your team: A thorough review of social media, including its pros, cons, various technological aspects and user expectations is absolutely critical for anyone that tweets in the name of an elected official, including the elected official herself. Appropriate training is the best way to avoid a major mistake, be it things that you should avoid tweeting (like claims of victory before you actually win, like the would-be Senator Joe Miller), how to tell the difference between a Direct Message and @ response (see former Congressman Anthony Weiner and Congressman Steve Cohen), when information that you think is private is actually public (like China's Xie Zhiqiang) and what buttons you can click on to avoid a massive negative backlash (like Rick Perry's team failing to disable the "like" function on YouTube). An important point here is that the training must be comprehensive. It must deal with how a platform works and what you can and cannot say. A simple review of these aspects of any social network can go a long way towards preventing a disaster.

Have a no-no list: Every elected official's social media team should have a list of subjects that they absolutely, positively refuse to talk about or mention. This list should have two parts:

1) Standard: Some things should be avoided regardless of who the elected official is. These include jokes about sex or that contain sexism (like the team of Senator Mitch McConnell), racism (Rob Towle, Chair of the Rutland Maine Republican Party and Progress Kentucky, the failed Kentucky Super PAC), references

to violence and revolutions (Kenneth Cole). Cursing, alcohol and drugs are also examples of things that should never be referred to, unless you are talking about a specific public policy matter.

2) Specific: Each elected official will have certain subjects that they don't want to touch upon. For example, it would be inappropriate for an elected official who had an affair or was accused of sexual impropriety to condemn another for doing the same. If a politician had previously been accused of anti-Semitism, then anti-Israel statements would be something to avoid. Make sure that your entire social media team knows what topics they should never push.

Use Social Media Management programs carefully: A social media management program, like Hootsuite or TweetDeck, can be absolutely critical for any professional using social media. The ability to monitor keywords (like an elected official's name or important issues), schedule tweets and manage multiple accounts can dramatically enhance your social media impact. However, inappropriate use can be a recipe for disaster. The NRA found that out the hard way when they went on auto-pilot and scheduled a tweet that read "Good morning, shooters!" in the aftermath of a mass shooting. If you use a social media management program, you can't just walk away; you have to make sure that you know what tweets are scheduled and delete them if world events insist on it. As an example, let's say that, God forbid, terrorists tried to kill the President. It would be bad form if an automatically scheduled tweet from the political opposition went out an hour later, attacking the President on some policy stance.

Social media management programs can also lead to confusion about what account is being tweeted from. As was seen in an entire section of this book (Wrong Account: Tweets that were meant for elsewhere), it is all too easy for a staffer who has linked their personal and professional accounts to confuse the two and get themselves into deep, deep trouble (as was the case Congressman Raul Labrador's former spokesman, Steve Hardy, who was fired after a risqué tweet that literally lasted fourteen seconds before it was deleted).

Establish a Social Media Policy and Plan: A policy is vitally necessary for many reasons. First, from an HR perspective, you have to have something that can cover your office in the event that someone commits a mistake that is so egregious it requires discipline or a firing. However, a good plan is more than legality and logistics. A social media policy should be proactive and discuss how a social media account will be governed, who is responsible, what kind of content will be created and disseminated and how feedback will be dealt with. As we saw in the case of Governor Mike Pence (R-IN), a good policy can lay the groundwork for what comments are appropriate and what aren't. Examples of areas that should be addressed in a social media policy include:

- Goals: Why are you on social media? What are you looking to accomplish with your presence there? This is an important question, as the rest of your social media plan will flow from the answer to this. Are you looking to connect better with constituents and seek their feedback? Get information out on your various legislative efforts? Brand yourself as an expert in a particular area of public policy? Sure, you want to do all of these things to some extent, but it's best to pick one or two areas and really concentrate on them than try to do everything.

- Staffing: Who will monitor the account and how often will they monitor it? If an account is monitored jointly by multiple staffers, or by staffers and the elected official, who will respond? When will they respond?

- Content: What type of content should be created and/or distributed? How often will the accounts be used and how frequently will they be monitored?

- Feedback: How will positive and negative feedback be handled? Under what circumstances is it acceptable to delete a comment or block a user? What are the expectations for how quickly feedback or comments will be addressed? How will this information reach the users of your social media? What will you do in the event of a crisis situation?

Double check everything: This goes for every post, link and retweet. You'd be amazed at how many typos or poor English uses (see "refudiate" by former Governor Palin) can be crammed into a 140 character tweet or a Facebook post. Always proofread your social media for poor grammar and always check where links are going. As we saw in the cases of Jill Bader (spokeswoman for Wisconsin Governor Walker, who made a debatably racist tweet at President Obama because she didn't check where her link pointed to), Sarah Pompei (spokeswoman for Meg Whitman, candidate for California governor, who tweeted a link that featured an Asian transvestite playing the bass instead of an endorsement from police officers), and Rob Wilson (British Member of Parliament who tweeted a link to a porn site instead of a blog post), even links from trusted friends can point people in directions you don't want them to go.

Last measure of defense: Think twice before you hit send or post. Is there any reason you don't want to say what you are about to say on social media? Any potential people you could offend that you don't want to (like Celebrity Boutique not checking to see why "Aurora" was trending before they tweeted)? Anything in that post that could come back to haunt you in a later campaign? Any potential security breaches (like Michigan's Congressman Hoekstra, who tweeted his location while in a war zone)? A moment's thought can stop years of grief.

Remember: Digital is forever and anything you say can go public in an instant. The experiences of Colleen Lachowicz (Maine State Senator and avid World of Warcraft player) and Jon Favreau (former Obama staffer who was photographed groping a cardboard cutout of Hillary Clinton) taught us that digital is forever and privacy is dead. Anything that is in a digital format can be disseminated world-wide in an instant. Any comment or picture can ruin a career in a moment. What's the best solution? To live as a hermit? Of course not, but public officials or candidates for office simply have to remember a golden rule: we are held to a higher standard. Like it or not, when you become a public official, your right to and expectation of anonymity vanish. Don't want to be photographed at a party? Don't go. Don't want people to see what you are tweeting on your "private" account? Don't tweet it.

That covers how to prevent a scandal or crisis; but again, no matter how hard you prepare, these things happen. Each scandal is different but generally speaking, it's best to address an ongoing and evolving crisis by using the following steps:

Immediate reaction: delete, acknowledge and apologize: First, if appropriate, delete the offensive content. You need to make sure that you acknowledge that you made a deletion in your apology, so as to not have people think that you deleted something in an effort to cover-up. It's appropriate to delete the content to recognize that you did something wrong.

Next, acknowledge and apologize. To demonstrate this, contrast the initial statements of KitchenAid (when an off-brand tweet attacked President Obama and his dead grandmother) and Bob Rucho (North Carolina Senator who said Obamacare was worse than Nazis, Soviets & terrorism).

KitchenAid acknowledged that they made an error ("irresponsible tweet") and offered their "deepest apologies." That's a lot of contrition packed into 140 characters. In contrast, Bob Rucho dug himself in harder by defending his obnoxious statement and adding a touch of arrogance to it by adding, "But surely you knew that." Rucho never did apologize for his initial statement.

Subsequent reaction - take personal responsibility and explain what happened, with no excuses:

Let's go back to the KitchenAid mistake. There was the immediate apology that was issued eight minutes after the errant tweet. A subsequent apology that came out within three hours expanded on the original apology:

Hello, everyone. My name is Cynthia Soledad, and I am the head of the KitchenAid brand.

I would like to personally apologize to President @ BarackObama, his family and everyone on Twitter for the offensive tweet sent earlier.

It was carelessly sent in error by a member of our Twitter team who, needless to say, won't be tweeting for us anymore.

That said, I take full responsibility for my team. Thank you for hearing me out.

This is an outstanding apology on many fronts:

- It contains an unreserved admission of guilt and apology to all offended, including the President.

- It explains what happens and, in generic terms, describes the consequences to the guilty party.

- There is a personal assumption of responsibility from the highest levels of KitchenAid.

A similar statement was sent to the media in a press release.

Contrast this statement to Progress Kentucky. Their initial and subsequent response when they made blatantly racist accusations against the Asian wife of Senator Mitch McConnell? They acknowledged that their tweets "may have crossed the line" but then said that it was fair to "question whether or not there's a conflict of interest." In other words, they were racist but thought it was fair. So they gave a half apology and then undercut it by defending their behavior.

Respond on the medium where you made the error: When attacked on Facebook, it may be tempting to avoid the medium completely. This is the worst strategy you can take. After all, in this example, the bulk of the people who saw what you did will likely still be listening on the same medium. Take the case of KitchenAid again. Their first apology occurred on Twitter, and then they tweeted out a link to their full apology statement.

Transparency rules: There is a golden rule in political scandals: the cover-up is worse than the crime. Transparency is key. Be prepared to answer every question truthfully, no matter how unflattering the answer, because eventually, the truth will probably come out anyway. The more open and honest you can be, the better.

Be ready to get yelled at and don't censor: If you have a full-blown apology statement, you always want to put it on social media. Inevitably, you will get nasty comments. Do not delete those comments unless they violate an easily accessible social media policy. As we saw in the case of Indiana Governor Mike Pence, censorship will get you nowhere except into more trouble. You want those comments to be located on the same thread as your apology. This is for a few reasons:

- It makes it easier to track negative comments and respond, if appropriate.

- It gives your defenders and supporters a chance to defend and support you. One of the great things about social media is that it allows others to leap to your defense and become your missionaries. A dedicated thread to a scandal makes it easier for your supporters to keep track of the attacks on you.

- It creates a pressure valve. If you have a scandal, it's better for all the feedback to be channeled into one comment thread rather than splayed across your entire wall. This means that you can continue to use Facebook in a positive manner to discuss other ongoing initiatives. At the same time, it decreases the chances that these threads will be hijacked by commenters who want to talk about the scandal.

Instruct your staff: If you screw up on social media, you will probably get calls to your office about the mistake. Make sure that your front line staff (the ones who answer the phones and the door) know what happened and how to address the issue. A summary should be prepared, complete with bullets on the issue, your response, your apology and answers to likely questions. You have to keep your staff informed, lest they are taken by surprise or say something that they shouldn't.

Review and adjust: In the aftermath of a social media scandal or screw up, a thorough review is required when the dust has settled. What happened? Why did it happen? What changes can you make to ensure that it doesn't happen again? What additional training is needed? Do you need additional oversight? Was your social media policy appropriately prepared for the issue? These are some of the questions that you must be prepared to answer in the aftermath of a scandal.

By now, if you are an elected official, candidate or staffer, you may be scared to death of ever tweeting again. The consequences for a social media screw-up can be devastating: a lost election, a lost job or worse. So what is an elected official to do? Never tweet again? Cut the cables to their office internet? Go back to simply holding "Ye ole Town Hall" meetings and rely exclusively on snail mail?

Take a look at most of the mistakes covered here. Some of them were a simple matter of carelessness: the wrong button touched, someone being in a rush and failing to double check a link, etc. Many of them demonstrated astounding lapses in judgment. But there's a key point that you shouldn't miss. Social media doesn't necessarily cause people to be stupid. Rather, it gives stupid people another arena in which they can be stupid. That is an absolutely critical concept to understand because the inverse is also true. If you have sound judgment, you will probably benefit significantly from extensive social media use.

Look at some of the things discussed in this book. Sure, Sarah Palin could have avoided her embarrassing use of the word "refudiate" if she had double checked her tweets. But really, was Palin ever known for her command of the English language and articulate speech? Yes, Anthony Weiner may have avoided a scandal had he simply responded to a tweet via a Direct Message instead of a public response, but if he was already texting random women racy pictures of himself, isn't it safe to say that his judgment clearly wasn't serving him?

At the end of the day, these stories can be outstanding parables for learning how to avoid the previous mistakes of elected official. But look at all the benefits. More than 25 percent of people regularly get their news for social media and more than 50 percent of people have learned about breaking news the same way. An astounding 70 percent of all 14-30 year olds get their news from social media. In other words, people are increasingly relying on social media to get their news, communicate with others and stay connected to their community.

What kind of foolish elected official would avoid using such a popular method of communication? Social media is a gold mine. It provides a non-stop, easily accessible way for elected officials to connect with their constituents, and vice versa. You have to use social media; governance is rapidly reaching a point where it is no longer avoidable.

Sure, social media use for elected officials can be tricky and comes with pitfalls. But it's not as if exploring new methods of communication is new to politicians. How do you think Warren Harding felt when he became the first President to speak on the radio? Or Franklin Roosevelt, when he became the first President to give a televised address?

New media is nothing new to politics. Only a fool avoids it; but the smart politician learns its new rules and how to best take advantage of it.

ॐ ૩ ॐ ૩

BIBLIOGRAPHY

Angelowicz, Ami. "Meet The World's Most Idiotic Teacher, Carly McKinney (NSFW)." The Frisky. N.p., 31 Jan. 2013. Web. 28 Dec. 2013. <http://www.thefrisky.com/2013-01-31/meet-the-worlds-most-idiotic-teacher-carly-mckinney-nsfw/>.

"Congress and Social Media: Use of Twitter and Facebook by Senators and Congressmen." Piper Report. N.p., 15 Apr. 2013. Web. 28 Dec. 2013. <http://www.piperreport.com/blog/2013/04/15/congress-social-media-twitter-facebook-senators-congressmen/>.

Yardley, William. "Alaska Winner, Lover of Privacy, Loses His Own." New York Times 3 Oct. 2010: n. pag. Alaska Winner, Lover of Privacy, Loses His Own. Web. 1 June 2013.

"Lessons from Lisa." The Magazine for People in Politics. N.p., n.d. Web. 1 June 2010. <http://www.campaignsandelections.com/print/303362/lessons-from-lisa.thtml>.

McCormick, John. "Murkowski Says She Will Run as Write-In Candidate in Senate Race in Alaska." Bloomberg.com. Bloomberg, 18 Sept. 2010. Web. 1 June 2013. <http://www.bloomberg.com/news/2010-09-18/murkowski-says-she-will-run-as-write-in-candidate-in-senate-race-in-alaska.html>.

"Miller v. Campbell." Wikipedia. Wikimedia Foundation, 24 July 2013. Web. 10 Sept. 2013. <http://en.wikipedia.org/wiki/Miller_v._Campbell>.

"State of Alaska 2010 General Election Official Results." Alaska Elecctions. N.p., n.d. Web. 2 June 2010. <http://www.elections.alaska.gov/results/10GENR/data/res ultsWI.pdf>.

Weber, Christopher. "Joe Miller Gets Ahead of Himself, Tweets About Picking Office Furniture in D.C.." Politics Daily. N.p., n.d. Web. 2 June 2010. <http://www.politicsdaily.com/2010/09/30/joe-miller-gets-ahead-of-himself-tweets-about-picking-office-fu/>.

Weber, Christopher. "Joe Miller Gets Ahead of Himself, Tweets About Picking Office Furniture in D.C.." Politics Daily. N.p., n.d. Web. 2 June 2010. <http://www.politicsdaily.com/2010/09/30/joe-miller-gets-ahead-of-himself-tweets-about-picking-office-fu/>.

Heine, Christopher. "A Week After Aurora: NRA Dark on Twitter, Celeb Boutique Prolific." AdWeek. N.p., 27 July 2012. Web. 29 Oct. 2013. <http://www.adweek.com/news/technology/week-after-aurora-nra-dark-twitter-celeb-boutique-prolific-142244>.

Klapper, Ethan. "NRA Tweet: Pro-Gun Group Sends Out Unfortunate Message After Aurora Shooting (UPDATED)." The Huffington Post. TheHuffingtonPost.com, 20 July 2012. Web. 20 July 2013. <http://www.huffingtonpost.com/2012/07/20/nra-tweet_n_1689862.html>

Balingit, Moriah. "Pittsburgh Mayor Ravenstahl cites 'grueling demands' in withdrawal from race." Pittsburgh Post-Gazette 13 Mar. 2013.

Heyl, Eric. "Mayor Ravenstahl's facade drops in social media remarks." Pittsburgh Tribune 10 May 2013: 2. TribLive. Web. 16 July 2013.

Lord, Rich. "Urban Development Boss Pat Ford Resigns."
Pittsburgh Post-Gazette 27 Aug. 2008: 2.

Mayo, Bob. "Pittsburgh Mayor Luke Ravenstahl's former
police bodyguard goes before grand jury." WTAE. N.p., 18
June 2013. Web. 16 July 2013.
<http://www.wtae.com/news/local/allegheny/pittsburgh-
mayor-luke-ravenstahls-former-police-bodyguard-going-
before-grand-jury-today/-/10927008/20614056/-/12pt0f3/-
/index.html>.

McNulty, Tim. "Mayor defends use of SUV; U.S. attorney to
review it." Pittsburgh Post-Gazette 3 Oct. 2007: 2. Print.

"Office of Mayor Luke Ravenstahl · About the Mayor." Office
of Mayor Luke Ravenstahl · About the Mayor. N.p., n.d.
Web. 15 July 2013.
<http://pittsburghpa.gov/mayor/about_the_mayor>.

"PA State Primary Election Results."WTAE. N.p., 21 May
2013. Web. 7 Nov. 2013.
<http://www.wtae.com/news/politics/pa-state-primary-
election-results/-/9680976/20225232/-/5j7mk4z/-
/index.html>.

Rotstein, Gary. "Mayor defends his golf outing." Pittsburgh
Post-Gazette 22 Aug. 2007: 2. Print

ABC57 News. ABC57. 29 Jan. 2014. Web. Transcript.

ABC57 News. ABC57. 23 Jun. 2014. Web. Transcript.

Blasko, Erin &Buckley, Madeline. "Councilman responds to
critics of graphic Facebook post." South Bend Tribune 2 Feb.
2013: n. pag. South Bend Tribune. Web. 4 Feb. 2013.

Blasko, Erin &Buckley, Madeline. "Councilman responds to
critics of graphic Facebook post." South Bend Tribune 28
Jan. 2014: n. pag. South Bend Tribune. Web. 4 Feb. 2014.

FOX28 Evening News. FOX28. 14 Feb. 2002. Web.
Transcript.

WSBT22 Evening News. WSBT22. 31 Jan. 2014. Television.

"VIDEO (WARNING - GRAPHIC LANGUAGE): Police camera shows Henry Davis Jr. traffic stop." South Bend Tribune. South Bend Tribune, 20 June 2013. Web. 4 Feb. 2013. <http://www.southbendtribune.com/video-warning---graphic-language-police-camera-shows-henry/video_a25da278-d99f-11e2-8467-001a4bcf6878.html>.

WNDUNews. WNDU. 12 Feb. 2014. Web. Transcript.

Edwards, Breann. "Rep. Steve Cohen tweet reveals secret daughter." POLITICO. N.p., 14 Feb. 2013. Web. 14 Aug. 2013. <http://www.politico.com/story/2013/02/woman-cohen-tweeted-is-daughter-87694.html>.

Marquez, Miguel. "'New Day' Exclusive: DNA test proves congressman not model's father." CNN Political Ticker. CNN, 18 July 2013. Web. 14 Aug. 2013. <http://politicalticker.blogs.cnn.com/2013/07/18/cnn-dna-test-proves-congressman-not-models-father/>.

"ActBlue" Support a Gamer Who's Under Attack." ActBlue. N.p., n.d. Web. 22 May 2013. <https://secure.actblue.com/page/santiaga>.

Calder, Amy. "Lachowicz unseats Martin in Senate District 25." Morning Sentinel [Augusta] 7 Nov. 2012: n. pag. Lachowicz unseats Martin in Senate District 25. Web. 21 May 2013.

"Public Campaign Finance Page for the State of Maine." Maine Commission on Governmental Ethics and Election Practices. State of Maine, n.d. Web. 19 May 2013. <http://www.mainecampaignfinance.com/public/entity_list.asp?TYPE=CAN&YEAR=2012>.

Schreier, Jason. "Maine Democrat is Supposedly Unfit For Office Because She Loves 'Poisoning and Stabbing' in World of Warcraft." Kotaku. N.p., 4 Oct. 2012. Web. 19 May 2013.

<http://kotaku.com/5948987/maine-democrat-is-supposedly-unfit-for-office-because-she-loves-poisoning-and-stabbing-in-world-of-warcraft>.

"Senator Colleen Lachowicz - Statement on Attacks." Senator Colleen Lachowicz. N.p., n.d. Web. 20 May 2013. <http://www.colleenlachowicz.com/?p=106>.

Stone, Matthew. "Ethics commission clears World of Warcraft candidate of wrongdoing." Bangor Daily News 1 Nov. 2012.

"CBS News." Altaffer, Mary. CBS News. CBS. 20 July 2012. Television.

Neiwert, David. "Sarah Palin tries to lie her way out of 'refudiate' coinage | Crooks and Liars." Crooks and Liars. N.p., 28 Dec. 2010. Web. 3 July 2013. <http://crooksandliars.com/david-neiwert/sarah-palin-tries-lie-her-way-out-re>.

"Park51." Wikipedia. Wikimedia Foundation, 11 Feb. 2013. Web. 1 Aug. 2013. <http://en.wikipedia.org/wiki/Park51>.

Tanabe, Karin. "Sarah Palin knocks conservationists." Politico. N.p., 27 Dec. 2010. Web. 1 July 2013. <http://www.politico.com/click/stories/1012/palin_knocks_conservationists_page2.html>.

Wilkie, Christina. "Sarah Palin's 'refudiate' wins Oxford dictionary's Word of the Year." TheHill. N.p., 16 Nov. 2010. Web. 4 July 2010. <http://thehill.com/capital-living/in-the-know/129309-sarah-palins-refudiate-wins-oxford-dictionarys-word-ofthe-year->.

AP. "School board member Gregory Beck resigns over Newtown comment." KNXV. KNXV, 9 Jan. 2014. Web. 5 Feb. 2014. <http://www.abc15.com/dpp/news/national/school-board-member-gregory-beck-resigns-over-newtown-comment>.

Boyd, Aaron. "Ethics Tosses Compaints After Beck Officially Resigns from Board of Ed." Brookfield Patch. N.p., 9 Jan. 2014. Web. 5 Feb. 2014.
<http://brookfield.patch.com/groups/politics-andelections/p/ethics-tosses-compaints-after-beck-officially-resigns-from-board-of-ed>.

"Evening News." NBC Conneticut Evening News. NBC Conneticut. 20 Nov. 2013. Web. Transcript.

Hutson, Nanci. "Embattled Brookfield BOE member resigns." The News-Times [Danbury] 7 Jan. 2014: n. pag. Newstimes.com. Web. 5 Feb. 2014.

AP. "Arkansas Supreme Court reassigns judge's cases." SFGate. N.p., 24 Mar. 2014. Web. 2 Apr. 2014.
<http://www.sfgate.com/news/article/Arkansas-Supreme-Court-reassigns-judge-s-cases-5344989.php>.

AP. "Arkansas judge fined in campaign-gifts case." The Washington Times. N.p., 28 June. 2014.
Web. 3 Jul. 2014.
<http://www.washingtontimes.com/news/2014/jun/28/arkansas-judge-fined-in-campaign-gifts-case/?utm_source=RSS_Feed&utm_medium=RSS>.

Brantley, Max. "Arkansas Blog." Arkansas Times. N.p., 5 Mar. 2014. Web. 1 Apr. 2014.
<http://www.arktimes.com/ArkansasBlog/archives/2014/03/05/judge-mike-maggio-withdraws-from-court-of-appeals-race-acknowledges-web-postings>.

"Daily Kos." Arkansas Judge Mike Maggio Outed for Racist, Sexist, Homophobic Posts. N.p., 10 Mar. 2014. Web. 2 Apr. 2014.
<http://www.dailykos.com/story/2014/03/10/1283494/-Arkansas-Judge-Mike-Maggio-Outed-for-Racist-Sexist-Homophobic-Posts#>.

"Honorable Mike Maggio." Arkansas Courts. N.p., n.d. Web. 1 Apr. 2014.

<https://courts.arkansas.gov/directories/circuit-judges/hon-mike-maggio>.

ArkansasOnline. "Maggio to be suspended, barred from judicial office under agreement."

Arkansas Democratic-Gazette [Little Rock] 6 Aug. 2014: n. pag. Arkansas

"Doctor's X-ray postings unsettling." Topeka Constitution-Journal 22 Feb. 2014: 0. cjonline.com. Web. 3 Apr. 2014.

Hohmann, James. "POLITICO." POLITICO. N.p., 23 Feb. 2014. Web. 3 Apr. 2014.
<http://www.politico.com/story/2014/02/kansas-candidate-posted-grisly-images-103817.html?hp=f2>.

Martin, Jonathan. "Lacking a House, a Senator Is Renewing His Ties in Kansas." New York Times 7 Feb. 2014: n. pag. New York Times. Web. 3 Apr. 2014.

"Pat Roberts (R-VA) Readies War on Doctors." Milton Wolf for U.S. Senate. Milton Wolf for U.S. Senate, 22 Feb. 2014. Web. 3 Apr. 2014. <http://www.miltonwolf.com/pat-roberts-r-va-readies-waron-doctors/>.

Shabad, Rebecca. "Poll: Roberts numbers drop in Kansas." TheHill. N.p., 21 Feb. 2014. Web. 3 Apr. 2014.
<http://thehill.com/blogs/ballot-box/senate-races/198909-sen-roberts-could-face-tight-primary-race-in-kansas-poll>.

"2014 Unofficial Kansas Primary Election Results." 2014 Unofficial Kansas Primary Election Results. N.p., n.d. Web. 6 Sept. 2014. <http://www.sos.ks.gov/ent/kssos_ent.html>.

"Statement from Dr. Milton Wolf." Milton Wolf for U.S. Senate. N.p., 23 Feb. 2014. Web. 3 Apr. 2014. <http://www.miltonwolf.com/statement-from-dr-milton-wolf/>.

Donnelly, John. "Congressman Twitters an Iraq Security Breach." Roll Call. Roll Call, 6 Feb. 2011. Web. 6 Aug. 2013. <http://www.rollcall.com/news/73257-1.html?cqp=1>.

Horn, Leslie. "7 Ways to Screw Up Your Political Career on Twitter." PCMAG.com. PC Magazine, 11 July 2011. Web. 6 Aug. 2013. <http://www.pcmag.com/slideshow/story/266502/7-ways-to-screw-up-your-political-career-on-twitter/7>.

Ostrow, Adam. "Mashable." Mashable. Mashable, 16 Mar. 2009. Web. 10 Aug. 2013. <http://mashable.com/2009/03/16/twitter-growth-rate-versus-facebook/>.

"Pentagon reviewing security policy after Hoekstra's Twitter updates from Iraq." The Ann Arbor News 11 Feb. 2009: n. pag. MLive.com. Web. 6 Aug. 2013.

"Pete Joekstra." Wikipedia. Wikimedia Foundation, n.d. Web. 10 Nov. 2013. <http://en.wikipedia.org/wiki/Peter_Hoekstra#2010_gubern atorial_election>.

Rao, Leena. "Twitter Added 30 Million Users In The Past Two Months." TechCrunch. TechCrunch, 31 Oct. 2010. Web. 10 Nov. 2013. <http://techcrunch.com/2010/10/31/twitter-users/>.

"'I have a masters degree in communication': Republican candidate's bizarre speech becomes internet hit." The Daily Mail [London] 10 Sept. 2010: 1. Print.

Gauger, Jeff. "Jeff Gauger: Davison's rant was long on style but notably short on substance." The Canton Rep 13 Oct. 2010: n. pag. Cantonrep.com. Web. 25 July 2013.

"Phil Davison." Wikipedia. Wikimedia Foundation, n.d. Web. 26 July 2013. <http://en.wikipedia.org/wiki/Phil_Davison>.

"Tosh.0 - March 28, 2011." Tosh.0.Comedy Central. 28 Mar. 2011. Television.

Cook, John. "Most of Newt Gingrich's Twitter Followers Are Fake." Gawker. N.p., 1 Aug. 2011. Web. 10 Aug. 2013. <http://gawker.com/5826645/most-of-newt-gingrichs-twitter-followers-are-fake>.

Cook, John. "Update: Only 92% of Newt Gingrich's Twitter Followers Are Fake." Gawker. N.p., 2 Aug. 2011. Web. 2 Aug. 2013. <http://gawker.com/5826960/update-only-92-of-newt-gingrichs-twitter-followers-are-fake>.

"Gingrich top aides abandon campaign." CNN Political Ticker RSS. N.p., 10 June 2011. Web. 7 Aug. 2013. <http://politicalticker.blogs.cnn.com/2011/06/10/breaking-gingrich-campaign-aides-resigns/>.

"Gingrich: I'm Not Giving Up." The Marietta Daily Journal 31 July 2011: 3. Print.

Neumann, Jeff. "Newt Gingrich Brags About His Twitter Followers." Gawker. N.p., 1 Aug. 2011. Web. 10 Aug. 2013. <http://gawker.com/5826477/newt-gingrich-brags-about-his-twitter-followers>.

Page, Susan. "Poll: Will anti-Congress mood cause another 'wave' election?." USA Today [MacLean] 8 Aug. 2011: 2. Print.

Saenz, Arlette. "Newt Gingrich Campaign Pushes Back on Fake Twitter Followers Accusation." ABC News. ABC News Network, 2 Aug. 2011. Web. 5 Aug. 2013. <http://abcnews.go.com/blogs/politics/2011/08/newt-gingrich-campaign-pushes-back-on-fake-twitter-followers-accusation/>.

ADD: Mistler, Steve. "King on Collins: We've got a model senator here." Portland Press Herald 16 May 2014: n. pag. CentralMaine.com. Web. 6 Sept. 2014.

"Bureau of International Information Programs." U.S. Department of State. U.S. Department of State, n.d. Web. 23 June 2013. <http://www.state.gov/r/iip/>.

Hayward, John. "STATE DEPARTMENT BLOWS $630K BUYING FACEBOOK "LIKES"." Human Events 3 July 2013: n. pag. Human Events. Web. 1 Aug. 2013.

Hicks, Josh. "IG report: State Department spent $630,000 to increase Facebook "likes"." Washington Post 3 July 2013: 3. Print.

Sandmeyer, Ellie. "Fox's Baseless Attack On State Department Online Outreach." Media Matters. N.p., 3 July 2013. Web. 1 Aug. 2013. <http://mediamatters.org/blog/2013/07/03/foxs-baseless-attack-on-state-department-online/194737>.

Spero, Domani. "State Dept's $630,000 Social Media "Buying Fans" Campaign, a Success" But Where's the Love? Diplopundit. N.p., 20 June 2013. Web. 23 June 2013. <http://diplopundit.net/2013/06/20/state-depts-630000-social-media-buying-fans-campaign-a-success-but-wheres-the-love/>.

Sink, Justin. "Three congressional staffers canned after tweets reveal in-office partying." TheHill. N.p., 8 Dec. 2011. Web. 12 June 2013. <http://thehill.com/blogs/hillicon-valley/technology/198269-three-congressional-staffers-canned-after-tweets-reveal-in-office-partying->.

"Tweets from Congressional Staffers Describe OnJob Drinking in Office of Congressman Larsen." NW Daily Marker. N.p., 8 Dec. 2011. Web. 13 June 2013. <http://www.nwdailymarker.com/2011/12/tweets-from-congressional-staffers-describe-on-job-drinking-in-office-of-congressman-larsen/>.

Fry, Steve. "Ex-research attorney faces misconduct allegations in Kline tweeting incident." The Topeka Capitol-Journal. 3 Sept. 2013: n. pag. Ex-research attorney faces misconduct allegations in Kline tweeting incident. Web. 1 Oct. 2013.

"WIBW News - September 3, 2013." Montano, Liz. WIBW News. WIBW. 3 Sept. 2013. Web. Transcript.

"Kansas City News - August 8, 2013." Newton, Ryan. Kansas City News. KSNC. 13 Aug. 2013. Web. Transcript.

Fry, Steve. "Informal admonishment: Judges impose mildest sanction for Kline-inspired tweets" Topeka Capitol-Journal. 13 Jan 2013. <http://cjonline.com/news/2014-01-13/informal-admonishment-judges-impose-mildest-sanction-kline-inspired-tweets>7 March 2013.

"#Pencership." Pencership. N.p., n.d. Web. 10 July 2013. <http://pencership.com/>.

"Gov. Mike Pence's deleted gay marriage Facebook posts reveal thorny challenges." Indianapolis Star 28 June 2013: n. pag. Gov. Mike Pence's deleted gay marriage Facebook posts reveal thorny challenges. Web. 11 July 2013.

"Indiana Governor Mike Pence." Governor Pence: Connect with Social Media. State of Indiana, n.d. Web. 10 July 2013. <http://www.in.gov/gov/2586.htm>.

"Mike Pence on Civil Rights." Mike Pence on Civil Rights. OnTheIssues, n.d. Web. 10 July 2013. <http://www.ontheissues.org/in/Mike_Pence_Civil_Rights.htm>.

"The Blurred Lines Between Social Media and Censorship." Governing Sep. 2013: n. pag. Governing - Dispatch. Web. 12 July 2013.

"What we can learn from Indiana Governor Mike Pence's social media fail." Examiner.com. N.p., 28 June 2013. Web. 10 July 2013. <http://www.examiner.com/article/what-we-can-learn-from-indiana-governor-mike-pence-s-social-media-fail>.

"David Cameron in Twitter gaffe No 2." The Guardian [London] 22 Sept. 2013: 1. David Cameron in Twitter gaffe No 2. Web. 28 Sept. 2013.

"David Cameron joins Twitter." Twitter Developers. Twitter, n.d. Web. 28 Sept. 2013. <https://dev.twitter.com/media/twitter-moments/government/david-cameron-joins>.

O'Conner, Maureen. "Sarah Palin's 'Favorite' Tweet Is About Our 'Taliban Muslim Illegally Elected President'." Gawker. N.p., 4 Nov. 2010. Web. 28 Sept. 2013. <http://gawker.com/5681802/sarah-palins-favorite-tweet-is-about-our-taliban-muslim-illegally-elected-president>.

Kane, Paul. "Reid, Democrats Trigger 'Nuclear' Option; Eliminate Most Filibusters on Nominees." The Washington Post 22 Nov. 2013: n. pag. The Washington Post. Web. 20 Dec. 2013.

"Mary Voted To Kill The Filibuster Today." The Hayride. N.p., 21 Nov. 2013. Web. 22 Dec. 2013. <http://thehayride.com/2013/11/mary-voted-to-kill-the-filibuster-today/>.

Schultheis, Emily. "Bill Cassidy staffer tweets Mary Landrieu-Mussolini picture." Politico [Washington] 22 Nov. 2013: n. pag. Politico. Web. 21 Dec. 2013.

"Bob Rucho." Ballotpedia. Ballotpedia, n.d. Web. 20 Dec. 2013. <http://ballotpedia.org/Bob_Rucho>.

"Evening News." Time Warner Cable News. Time Warner Cable. 16 Dec. 2013. Web. Transcript.

Morrill, Jim. "Rucho defends controversial tweet." North Carolina News & Observer [Raleigh] 16 Dec. 2013: 1. Print.

"NC Gop Asks Lawmaker to Apologize for Nazi Tweet." ABCnews.co. ABC, 17 Dec. 2013. Web. 22 Dec. 2013.

<http://abcnews.go.com/US/wireStory/nc-gop-asks-lawmaker-apologize-nazi-tweet-21237734>.

"NC SBE Election Results" NC SBE Election Results. N.p., n.d. Web. 3 July 2014.
<http://enr.ncsbe.gov/ElectionResults/?election_dt=05/06/2 014>.

"State Senator Robert Rucho (R-NC) compares Obamacare to Nazis." Political Fails. N.p., 18 Dec. 2013. Web. 30 Dec. 2013.
<http://politicalfails.wordpress.com/2013/12/18/state-senator-robert-rucho-r-nc-compares-obamacare-to-nazis/>.

Wooston, Cleve. "State Sen. Rucho's tweet comparing Obamacare to America's wars sparks controversy." North Carolina News & Observer [Raleigh] 17 Dec. 2013: 1. Print.

Alman, Ashley. "State Lawmaker Calls Arizona A 'Desert Racist Wasteland' After Football Loss." The Huffington Post. TheHuffingtonPost.com, 22 Dec. 2013. Web. 26 Dec. 2013.
<http://www.huffingtonpost.com/2013/12/22/joe-fitzgibbon-arizona-racist_n_4491067.html>.

"Arizona SB 1070." Wikipedia. Wikimedia Foundation, n.d. Web. 26 Dec. 2013.
<http://en.wikipedia.org/wiki/Arizona_SB_1070>.

"Evening News." Daniels, Chris. King5 Evening News. NBC. KING5, Seattle. 23 Dec. 2013. Web. Transcript.

"Fitzgibbon." Rep. Joe Fitzgibbon. Washington Legislature, n.d. Web. 26 Dec. 2013.
<http://www.leg.wa.gov/house/representatives/pages/fitzgi bbon.aspx>.

Fitzgibbon, Joe. "Joe Fitzgibbon for State Representative." Facebook. Joe Fitzgibbon, 23 Dec. 2013. Web. 26 Dec. 2013.
<https://www.facebook.com/permalink.php?story_fbid=101 52048992718070&id=376773153069>.

"Chairman & CEO." Motion Picture Association of America. Motion Picture Association of America, n.d. Web. 1 Aug. 2013. <http://www.mpaa.org/about/ceo>.

Newell, Jim. "Sen. Chris Dodd's Statesmanlike Tweet: 'U love torturing me w this shit'." Gawker. N.p., 18 Nov. 2013. Web. 30 July 2013. <http://gawker.com/5693432/sen-chris-dodds-statesmanlike-tweet-u-love-torturing-me-w-this-shit>.

Pitney, Nico. "'Chris Dodd' Says 'Sh*t' On Twitter: The Funniest Reactions." The Huffington Post. TheHuffingtonPost.com, 18 Nov. 2010. Web. 1 Aug. 2013. <http://www.huffingtonpost.com/2010/11/18/chris-dodd-shit-twitter-senator-senchrisdodd_n_785437.html#s185701title=Evan_Hughes>.

"ShitMyDoddSays." Twitter. N.p., n.d. Web. 1 Aug. 2013. <https://twitter.com/ShitMyDoddSays>.

Chen, Joyce. "Secret Service Twitter feed posts tweet slamming Fox News just one week after creating account." New York Daily News 18 May 2011: n. pag. Daily News. Web. 3 Aug. 2013.

Khan, Huma. "Secret Service Employee Accidentally Tweets About "Blathering" While "Monitoring" Fox News." ABC News. ABC News Network, 18 May 2011. Web. 3 Aug. 2013. <http://abcnews.go.com/blogs/politics/2011/05/secret-service-employee-accidentally-tweets-about-blathering-while-monitoring-fox-news/>.

Levine, Mike. "No Secrets On Twitter: Secret Service Official Posts Tweet Taking Aim At Fox News." Fox News. Fox News Network, 18 May 2011. Web. 3 Aug. 2013. <http://www.foxnews.com/politics/2011/05/18/no-secrets-on-twitter-secret-service-official-posts-tweet-taking-aim-atfox/>.

"ShortFormBlog.Read a little.Learn a lot.." ShortFormBlog.
N.p., 11 May 2019. Web. 3 Aug. 2013.
<http://shortformblog.com/post/5612855107/secret-
service-fox-news>.

Helderman, Rosalind S. "Labrador Fires Spokesman over
Accidental Tweet." *The Washington Post* 7 Feb. 2013: 1.
Washington Post. Web. 5 Aug. 2013.

Popkey, Dan. "Longtime Labrador spokesman fired for
bawdy Super Bowl tweet." Idaho Statesman Blogs. The
Idaho Statesman, 13 Feb. 2013. Web. 4 Aug. 2013.
<http://blogs.idahostatesman.com/longtime-labrador-
spokesman-fired-for-bawdy-tweet/>.

Bernick, Bob & Davison, Lee. "Advertise with usReport this
ad Shurtleff drops out of U.S. Senate race." *Desert News*
[Salt Lake City] 5 Nov. 2009: n. pag. Desert News. Web. 8
Aug. 2013.

Gehrke, Robert. "Bennett out; GOP delegates reject 18-year
Senate veteran." *The Salt Lake Tribune* [Salt Lake City] 8
May 2010: n. pag. The Salt Lake Tribune. Web. 7 Aug.
2013.

Wauters, Robin. "Utah Attorney General Mark Shurtleff Uses
Twitter To Announce Execution." TechCrunch. N.p., 18 June
2010. Web. 8 Aug. 2013.
<http://techcrunch.com/2010/06/18/mark-shurtleff-
twitter/>.

"Congressman Chris Lee Resigns Following Gawker
Revelation." Gawker. N.p., 9 Feb. 2010. Web. 10 Aug. 2013.
<http://gawker.com/5756377/craigslist-congressman-
resigns>.

O'Connor, Maureen. "Married GOP Congressman Sent Sexy
Pictures to Craigslist Babe." Gawker. Gawker, 12 Feb. 2009.
Web. 10 Aug. 2013. <http://gawker.com/5755071/married-
gop-congressman-sent-sexy-pictures-to-craigslist-
babe?tag=craigslistcongressman>.

"Statement of Canvass." New York Board of Elections. New York Board of Elections, 25 May 2011. Web. 9 Aug. 2013. <http://www.elections.ny.gov/NYSBOE/elections/2011/Special/26CDSpecialVoteResults.pdf>.

Brown, Campbell. "Commentary: Clinton changes her tune on sexism." CNN. Cable News Network, 5 Dec. 2008. Web. 12 Aug. 2013. <http://www.cnn.com/2008/POLITICS/12/05/campbell.brown.clinton/#cnnSTCText>.

"Jon Favreau (speechwriter)." Wikipedia. Wikimedia Foundation, n.d. Web. 12 Aug. 2013. <http://en.wikipedia.org/wiki/Jon_Favreau_(speechwriter)>.

Malcolm, Andrew. "Top of the Ticket." Obama speechwriter photographed groping Hillary Clinton likeness. *Los Angeles Times*, 5 Dec. 2008. Web. 11 Aug. 2013. <http://latimesblogs.latimes.com/washington/2008/12/obama-favreau.html>.

"One More Question...." 44 - Politics & Policy in Obama's Washington. The Washington Post, 4 Dec. 2008. Web. 11 Aug. 2013. <http://voices.washingtonpost.com/44/2008/12/one-more-question.html>.

"Report: Every Potential 2040 President Already Unelectable Due To Facebook | Video | The Onion - America's Finest News Source." Report: Every Potential 2040 President Already Unelectable Due To Facebook | Video | The Onion - America's Finest News Source. The Onion, n.d. Web. 27 Dec. 2013. <http://www.theonion.com/video/report-every-potential-2040-president-already-unel,27963/>.

Bierschbach, Briana. "Mills outraises Nolan in 8th District race | Politics in Minnesota." Mills outraises Nolan in 8th District race Comments. Politics in Minnesota, 16 Oct. 2013. Web. 27 Dec. 2013.

<http://politicsinminnesota.com/2013/10/mills-outraises-nolan-in-8th-district-race/>.

Rupar, Aaron. "Stewart Mills, GOP congressional candidate, hits a beer bong [PHOTOS]." The Blotter. N.p., 22 Nov. 2013. Web. 27 Dec. 2013. <http://blogs.citypages.com/blotter/2013/11/stewart_mills_gop_congressional_hopeful_knows_how_to_party_photos.php>.

Chen, Li. "China's Anthony Weiner: Govt Official Mistakenly Woos Mistress on Weibo." Tech in Asia. N.p., 21 June 2011. Web. 14 Aug. 2013. <http://www.techinasia.com/sina-microblog-affair/>.

Hung, Huang. "China's Anthony Weiner." *The Daily Beast. Newsweek/Daily Beast*, 23 Sept. 2011. Web. 14 Aug. 2013. <http://www.thedailybeast.com/articles/2011/09/23/xie-zhiqiang-china-s-anthony-weiner.html>.

"Social Media Strikes Again: China's Weiner." China Real Time Report. *The Wall Street Journal*, 22 June 2011. Web. 15 Aug. 2013. <http://blogs.wsj.com/chinarealtime/2011/06/22/social-media-strikes-again-chinas-anthony-weiner/>.

Tsukayama, Hayley. "Chinese politician caught in social media scandal." *The Washington Post* [Washington] 22 June 2011: n. pag. Chinese politician caught in social media scandal. Web. 15 Aug. 2011.

"Lehigh County Election Results." Lehigh County Election Results. N.p., n.d. Web. 16 Aug. 2013. <http://www.lehighcounty.org/departments/voterregistration/electionresults/tabid/445/default.aspx>.

O'Hare, Bernie. "Lehigh Valley Ramblings." Who Are The Tony Phillips Screwdrivers?. N.p., 28 Jan. 2008. Web. 16 Aug. 2013. <http://lehighvalleyramblings.blogspot.com/2008/01/whoare-tony-phillips-screwdrivers.html>.

O'Hare, Bernie. "Lehigh Valley Ramblings." Tony Phillips: Lookin' For Love in All the Wrong Places. N.p., 9 Sept. 2009. Web. 15 Aug. 2013. <http://lehighvalleyramblings.blogspot.com/2009/09/tony-phillips-lookin-for-love-in-all.html>.

Renshaw, Jarrett. "Republican candidate may quit race after cybersex chat revealed." The Morning Call [Allentown] 9 Sept. 2009: n. pag. The Morning Call. Web. 17 Aug. 2013.

Renshaw, Jarrett. "Phillips' Facebook Chat mate Revealed." The Morning Call [Allentown] 16 Sept. 2009: n. pag. The Morning Call. Web. 17 Aug. 2013.

Bennett-Smith, Meredith. "Anthony Weiner Paid Private Investigator $43,100 To Look Into His Own Twitter Hacking Lies: Report." The Huffington Post. TheHuffingtonPost.com, 28 July 2013. Web. 21 Aug. 2013. <http://www.huffingtonpost.com/2013/07/28/anthony-weiner-private-investigator-twitter-hacking-lies_n_3667680.html>.

Bresnahan, John. "Nancy Pelosi calls for Anthony Weiner ethics inquiry." POLITICO. POLITICO, 7 June 2011. Web. 22 Aug. 2013. <http://www.politico.com/news/stories/0611/56365.html>.

Chen, David. "Congressman Pushes Staff Hard, or Out the Door." The New York Times 23 July 2008: n. pag. The New York Times. Web. 19 Aug. 2013.

"Congressman Weiner resigns." msnbc.com. N.p., 17 June 2013. Web. 31 Dec. 2013. <http://www.nbcnews.com/id/43425251/ns/politics-capitol_hill/#.UjRBIsakrl8>.

Corky Siemaszko , Alison Gendar, Reuven. "Weinergate: Cops probe Rep. Anthony Weiner's Tweets to minor, pol's team says it was G-rated." New York Daily News 11 June 2011: n. pag. New York Daily News. Web. 23 Aug. 2013.

Doll, Jen. "Anthony Weiner Nearly Doubles His Twitter Followers During Weinergate." The Voice Blogs. The Voice, 9 June 2011. Web. 19 Aug. 2013. <http://blogs.villagevoice.com/runninscared/2011/06/anthony_weiner_12.php>.

"Evening News." NBC News New York. WNBC. WNBC, New York. 7 June 2011. Web. Transcript.

Halfbringer, David. "Weiner's Record In House - Intensity, Publicity and Limited Results." *The New York Times* 12 June 2011: n. pag. The New York Times. Web. 22 Aug. 2013.

Hernandez, Raymond. "House Democrats Step Up Calls for Weiner to Quit." *New York Times* 8 June 2011: n. pag. New York Times. Web. 22 Aug. 2013.

Howard, Dylan. "Radar Online." Radar Online. N.p., 6 June 2011. Web. 22 Aug. 2013. <http://radaronline.com/exclusives/2011/06/weinergate-grows-another-woman-provides-sex-messages-his-account/>.

James Oliphant, Michael Memoli. "New half-naked photos: Rep. Weiner calls a news conference." *Los Angeles Times* 6 June 2011: 1. Print.

"President Obama's Twitter Account Hacked." InformationWeek. InformationWeek, 25 Mar. 2010. Web. 20 Aug. 2013. <http://www.informationweek.com/internet/security/president-obamas-twitter-account-hacked/224200349>.

"Rep. Weiner: I did not send Twitter crotch pic." CBSNews. CBS Interactive, 29 May 2011. Web. 21 Aug. 2013. <http://www.cbsnews.com/stories/2011/05/29/politics/main20067242.shtml>.

Senior, Jennifer. "Anthony Weiner's Big Ego." Daily Intelligencer. *New York Magazine*, 2 June 2011. Web. 19 Aug. 2013.

<http://nymag.com/daily/intelligencer/2011/06/anthony_w einers_big_ego.html>.

"Weiner 'can't say with certitude' that lewd photo isn't of him." NBC News. NBC News, 1 June 2011. Web. 21 Aug. 2013. <http://firstread.nbcnews.com/_news/2011/06/01/6764247 -weiner-cant-say-with-certitude-that-lewd-photo-isnt-of-him?lite>.

Barbaro, Michael. "All Puns Aside, Weiner Makes Lucrative Name in Consulting." *New York Times* 29 Apr. 2013: n. pag. The New York Times. Web. 22 Aug. 2013.

Campanile, Carl. "Weiner caught sending dirty messages and photos a year after his sexting scandal." *New York Post* 24 July 2013: 1. Print.

"EXCLUSIVE: Anthony Weiner Hasn't Changed Poor Huma Abedin, New Image Of His Penis." The Dirty. N.p., 22 July 2013. Web. 31 Dec. 2013. <http://thedirty.com/2013/07/exclusive-anthony-weiner-hasnt-changed-poor-huma-abedin-new-image-of-his-penis/>.

Edwards-Levy, Ariel. "Poll: Anthony Weiner's Numbers Plummet After New Scandal Revelations." The Huffington Post. TheHuffingtonPost.com, 25 July 2013. Web. 1 Sept. 2013. <http://www.huffingtonpost.com/2013/07/25/poll-anthony-weiner_n_3653422.html>.

"Election 2013." WNYC. WNYC, n.d. Web. 20 Sept. 2013. <http://project.wnyc.org/election2013/>.

Ellie Hall, Michael Rusch Andrew Kaczynski. "BuzzFeed." BuzzFeed. N.p., 23 July 2013. Web. 31 Dec. 2013. <http://www.buzzfeed.com/andrewkaczynski/here-is-the-woman-linked-to-anthony-weiner-in-sex-chats>.

Foley, Elise. "Nancy Pelosi: Anthony Weiner And Bob Filner Need To 'Get A Clue'." The Huffington Post.

TheHuffingtonPost.com, 25 July 2013. Web. 1 Sept. 2013.
<http://www.huffingtonpost.com/2013/07/25/nancy-pelosi-
anthony-weiner-bobfilner_n_3652966.html>.

Glueck, Katie. "POLITICO." POLITICO. N.p., 10 Sept. 2013.
Web. 15 Sept. 2013.
<http://www.politico.com/story/2013/09/sydney-leathers-
anthony-weiner-election-party-96588.html?hp=r3>.

Hernandez, Javier. "Weiner vs. Heckler at a Brooklyn
Bakery." *New York Times* 4 Sept. 2013: 1. Print.

Bacon, John & Camia, Catalina. "Anthony Weiner vows to
stay in NYC mayor's race." *USA Today* [Atlanta] 28 July
2013: n. pag. USA Today. Web. 1 Sept. 2013.

McAdams, Ashley. "Anthony Weiner Sees Bump In Polling
Numbers." The Huffington Post. TheHuffingtonPost.com, 28
May 2013. Web. 24 Aug. 2013.
<http://www.huffingtonpost.com/2013/05/28/anthony-
weiner-nycmayor_n_3347673.html>.

"New York City Mayoral Race." NBC New York. N.p., 26 June
2013. Web. 31 Dec. 2013.
<http://www.nbcnewyork.com/news/local/Anthony-Weiner-
Frontrunner-NYC-Mayoral-Race-Poll-Christine-Quinn-
213008841.html>.

"New York City mayoral election, 2013." Wikipedia.
Wikimedia Foundation, n.d. Web. 15 Sept. 2013.
<http://en.wikipedia.org/wiki/New_York_City_mayoral_elect
ion,_2013>.

Robillard, Kevin. "POLITICO." POLITICO. N.p., 22 May 2013.
Web. 23 Aug. 2013.
<http://www.politico.com/story/2013/05/anthony-weiner-
nyc-mayor-run-91721.html>.

Voorhees, Josh. "Anthony Weiner Ended His Failed
Campaign by Flipping Off a Reporter." Slate Magazine. N.p.,
11 Sept. 2013. Web. 15 Sept. 2013.

<http://www.slate.com/blogs/the_slatest/2013/09/11/antho
ny_weiner_ends_his_campaign_by_flipping_off_a_reporter.
html>.

"Weiner Admits Explicit Texting After House Exit." *The New
York Times* 23 July 2013: n. pag. New York Times. Web. 20
Sept. 2013.

"Weiner dodges sexting partner, flips the bird as he rides
off." CNN Political Ticker. CNN, 11 Sept. 2013. Web. 15
Sept. 2013.
<http://politicalticker.blogs.cnn.com/2013/09/11/weiner-
dodges-sexting-partner-flips-the-bird-as-he-rides-off/>.

"Evening News." CBS Evening News Connecticut. WTIC.
WTIC, Farmington. 18 July 2012. Web. Transcript.

McCullough, Jack. "Racism from the Rutland County
Republican Committee." Green Mountain Daily::. N.p., 15
July 2012. Web. 25 Aug. 2013.
<http://www.greenmountaindaily.com/diary/8948/racism-
from-the-rutland-county-republican-committee>.

"Rutland County, Vermont." Wikipedia.
Wikimedia Foundation, n.d. Web. 25 Aug. 2013.
<http://en.wikipedia.org/wiki/Rutland_County,_Vermont#Po
litics>.

"Vermont gubernatorial election, 2012." Wikipedia.
Wikimedia Foundation, n.d. Web. 26 Aug. 2013.
<http://en.wikipedia.org/wiki/Vermont_gubernatorial_electi
on,_2012>.

AP. "Minnesota: Quist tops Parry in Congressional primary."
LaCrosse Tribune 15 Aug. 2012: n. pag.
LaCrosseTribune.com. Web. 29 Aug. 2013.

"It takes a worried man: SD 26 GOP Endorsee Mike Parry
scrubs potentially offensive twitter posts - See more at:
http://www.bluestemprairie.com/bluestemprairie/2009/12/
mikeparryscrubstwitterposts.html#sthash.6joaFhHz.dpuf."

Bluestem Prairie. N.p., 9 Dec. 2009. Web. 27 Aug. 2010.
<http://www.bluestemprairie.com/bluestemprairie/2009/12/mikeparryscrubstwitterposts.html>.

Ostermeir, Eric. "Mike Parry Fends Off Critics, Engbrecht, and Srp to Hold 26th Senate District for GOP." Smart Politics. University of Minnesota, 27 Jan. 2010. Web. 27 Aug. 2013.
<http://blog.lib.umn.edu/cspg/smartpolitics/2010/01/mike_parry_fends_off_critics_e.php>.

"Remarks by the President at Reception Commemorating the Enactment of the Hate Crimes Prevention Act." Civil Rights Division Home Page. N.p., n.d. Web. 28 Aug. 2013.
<http://www.justice.gov/crt/about/crm/matthewshepard.php>.

Weiner, Rachel. "Mike Parry, Minnesota State Senate Candidate, Defends Racist Twitter Message." The Huffington Post. TheHuffingtonPost.com, 6 Jan. 2010. Web. 28 Aug. 2013. <http://www.huffingtonpost.com/2010/01/06/mike-parry-minnesota-stat_n_413200.html>.

"WFPL News." Bailey, Phillip. WFPL News. WFMP - 89.3. WFPL, Louisville. 26 Feb. 2013. Web. Transcript.

Botwinick, Nathaniel. "Liberal Kentucky Super PAC Attacks Mitch McConnell's 'Chinese' Wife | National Review Online." National Review Online. N.p., 26 Feb. 2013. Web. 31 Aug. 2013.
<http://www.nationalreview.com/corner/341619/liberal-kentucky-super-pac-attacks-mitch-mcconnells-chinese-wife-nathaniel-botwinick>.

"WMBF Evening News." Flack, Eric. WMBF Evening News. WMBF. WMBF, Myrtle Beach. 11 Apr. 2013. Web. Transcript.

Keyes, Scott. "Liberal Super PAC Sends Racist Tweet About Mitch McConnell's Chinese Wife." ThinkProgress. N.p., 26 Feb. 2013. Web. 23 Aug. 2013.

<http://thinkprogress.org/justice/2013/02/26/1642141/raci st-super-pac/>.

"Liberal Group Under Fire for Anti-Asian Racist Tweet."
DiversityInc. N.p., n.d. Web. 30 Aug. 2013.
<http://www.diversityinc.com/diversity-and-inclusion/what-
anti-asian-racist-tweet-did-liberal-political-group-use/>.

MCMORRIS-SANTORO , Evan. "Kentucky Progressive Group
Tweets Racist Conspiracy About Mitch McConnell's Wife."
Talking Points Memo. N.p., 13 Feb. 1926. Web. 30 Aug.
2013. <http://talkingpointsmemo.com/dc/kentucky-
progressive-group-tweets-racist-conspiracy-about-mitch-
mcconnell-s-wife>.

MCMORRIS-SANTORO, Evan. "Kentucky Democrats Call
Progressive PAC's Tweets "Deplorable"." Talking Points
Memo. N.p., 26 Feb. 2013. Web. 29 Aug. 2013.
<http://talkingpointsmemo.com/livewire/kentucky-
democrats-call-progressive-pac-s-tweets-deplorable>.

Montgomery, Lori. "Senate GOP blocks bill that would
promote less outsourcing." *The Washington Post* 28 Sept.
2010: 1. The Washington Post Business. Web. 1 Sept. 2013.

Rense, Jeff. "rense.com." rense.com. N.p., n.d. Web. 29
Aug. 2013. <http://www.rense.com/>.

Tau, Byron. "POLITICO." POLITICO. N.p., 12 Aug. 2013.
Web. 29 Aug. 2013.
<http://www.politico.com/story/2013/08/progress-
kentucky-closing-fec-95444.html>.

"Adviser to Puerto Rican Speaker of House Apologizes for
Anti-Obama Tweets, Then Blocks People." Latino Rebels.
N.p., 3 Aug. 2012. Web. 4 Sept. 2013.
<http://www.latinorebels.com/2012/08/03/adviser-to-
puerto-rican-speaker-of-house-apologizes-for-anti-obama-
tweets-then-blocks-people/>.

"Calls for Puerto Rico political aide to resign after she sent Obama tweet telling him to 'take Michelle to Burger King, buy her a sundae with double banana, take her to your homeland, Kenya!'." *Daily Mail* [London] 2 Aug. 2012: n. pag. MailOnline. Web. 3 Sept. 2013.

Coto, Danica. "theGrio." theGrio. Associated Press, 1 Aug. 2012. Web. 3 Sept. 2013. <http://thegrio.com/2012/08/01/puerto-rico-adviser-under-fire-for-racial-tweet-about-the-obamas/>.

Leal, Samantha. "Adviser to Puerto Rican Lawmaker Asked to Resign After Anti-Obama Tweet." Heidi Wys Adviser to Puerto Rico Lawmaker to Resign After Obama Tweet. Latina, 2 Aug. 2012. Web. 4 Sept. 2013. <http://www.latina.com/lifestyle/politics/heidi-wys-anti-barack-obama-tweet-resignation-puerto-rico#axzz2g7OphLRF>.

Wing, Nick. "Heidi Wys, Adviser To Powerful Puerto Rico Lawmaker, Faces Calls To Resign After Anti-Obama Tweet." The Huffington Post. TheHuffingtonPost.com, 1 Aug. 2012. Web. 2 Sept. 2013. <http://www.huffingtonpost.com/2012/08/01/heidi-wys-obama-tweet-puerto-rico_n_1729377.html>.

"Wys has regrets over her anti-Obama tweets." Caribbean Business. N.p., 2 Aug. 2012. Web. 4 Sept. 2013.

Cooper, Michael. "More U.S. Rail Funds for 13 States as 2 Reject Aid." *New York Times* 9 Dec. 2010: n. pag. New York Times. Web. 6 Sept. 2013.

Fox 11 Evening News. Fox11. 23 Sept. 2010. Web. Transcript.

"Evening News." News. WTMJ. 17 Aug. 2012. Web. Transcript.

AP. "AP poll: U.S. majority have prejudice against blacks."
USA Today [Atlanta] 27 Oct. 2012: n. pag. USA Today. Web.
10 Dec. 2013.

"Discrimination Against Latin Americans." Do Something.
N.p., n.d. Web. 10 Dec. 2013.
<http://www.dosomething.org/tipsandtools/discrimination-against-latin-americans>.

Elving, Ron. "RNC Post-Election Report A Line In The Sand
For Divided GOP." NPR. NPR, 19 Mar. 2013. Web. 11 Dec.
2013.
<http://www.npr.org/blogs/itsallpolitics/2013/03/18/17468
9113/rnc-chairs-postmortem-report-a-line-in-the-sand-for-divided-gop>.

Killough, Ashley. "RNC clarifies tweet that suggests racism is
over." CNN Political Ticker. CNN, 2 Dec. 2013. Web. 12 Dec.
2013. <http://politicalticker.blogs.cnn.com/2013/12/02/rnc-clarifies-tweet-that-suggests-racism-is-over/>.

Moore, Martha. "GOP tries new minority outreach
campaign." *USA Today* [Atlanta] 16 Aug. 2013: 1. Print.

Schlutheis, Emily. "Exit polls 2012: How President Obama
won." POLITICO. N.p., 7 Nov. 2012. Web. 11 Dec. 2013.
<http://www.politico.com/news/stories/1112/83461.html>.

"Dad's Army." Wikipedia. Wikipedia, n.d. Web. 21 Dec.
2013. <http://en.wikipedia.org/wiki/Dad%27s_Army>.

Geoghegan, Tom. "How offensive is the word 'pikey'?." BBC
News. BBC, 6 Nov. 2008. Web. 20 Dec. 2013.
<http://news.bbc.co.uk/2/hi/uk_news/magazine/7446274.st
m>.

Lyons, James. "David Cameron's Downing Street Twitter
account follows escort service Check out all the latest News,
Sport & Celeb gossip at Mirror.co.uk
http://www.mirror.co.uk/news/uk-news/david-camerons-downing-street-twitter-2814113#ixzz2pANmKQ3u "The

Mirror [London] 20 Nov. 2013: n. pag. MirrorNews. Web. 20 Dec. 2013.

Prynne, Miranda. "MP Jack Dromey accused of racism after using word 'pikey'." *The Telegraph* [London] 13 Dec. 2013: n. pag. The Telegraph. Web. 21 Dec. 2013.

Syal, Rajeev. "Labour MP Jack Dromey warned over Royal Mail 'pikey' comment." *The Guardian* [London] 13 Dec. 2013: n. pag. Labour MP Jack Dromey warned over Royal Mail 'pikey' comment. Web. 20 Dec. 2013.

Giroux, Greg. "Business Week." Republicans Give Party F for Minorities Seeking to Belong. Bloomberg News, 19 Aug. 2012. Web. 22 Dec. 2013. <http://www.businessweek.com/news/2012-08-29/republicans-give-party-f-for-minorities-seeking-to-belong#p1>.

Glueck, Katie. "POLITICO." POLITICO. N.p., 3 Dec. 2013. Web. 21 Dec. 2013. <http://www.politico.com/story/2013/12/scott-walker-aide-fired-100611.html>.

Phillip, Abby. "Gov. Walker Urges Parents to Skip Toys and Send the Christmas Money to Him." ABC News. ABC News Network, 3 Dec. 2013. Web. 22 Dec. 2013. <http://abcnews.go.com/blogs/politics/2013/12/gov-walker-urges-parents-to-skip-toys-and-send-the-christmas-money-to-him/>.

"Daily Kos." Indiana A.G. fires deputy Jeff Cox over blog posts. N.p., 23 Feb. 2011. Web. 16 July 2013. <http://www.dailykos.com/story/2011/02/23/948880/-Indiana-A-G-fires-deputy-Jeff-Cox-over-blog-posts#>.

Popkin, Helen. "Indiana official loses job after 'live ammo' tweet." NBC News. N.p., 23 Feb. 2011. Web. 15 July 2013. <http://www.nbcnews.com/technology/indiana-official-loses-job-after-live-ammo-tweet-124977>.

Gettys, Travis. "NH Republican mocks domestic violence victims in sexually suggestive Facebook post | The Raw Story." NH Republican mocks domestic violence victims in sexually suggestive Facebook post | The Raw Story. N.p., 11 Mar. 2014. Web. 30 Mar. 2014. <http://www.rawstory.com/rs/2014/03/11/nh-republican-mocks-domestic-violence-victims-in-sexually-suggestive-facebook-post/>.

"Rep. Kyle Tasker: '50,000 battered women and I still eat mine plain'." Rep. Kyle Tasker: '50,000 battered women and I still eat mine plain'. N.p., 10 Mar. 2014. Web. 30 Mar. 2014. <http://miscellanyblue.com/post/79199364298>.

Ronayne, Kathleen. "N.H. Rep. Kyle Tasker says "battered women Facebook post misconstrued." *Concord Monitor* 13 Mar. 2013: n. pag. Concord Monitor. Web. 29 Mar. 2013.

"WMUR Evening News." WMUR Evening News. WMUR. 27 Feb. 2013. Web. Transcript.

"Democratic Party of Sacramento County » Democratic Party of Sacramento County Calls For and Accepts Resignation of Communications Chair." Democratic Party of Sacramento County RSS. Democratic Party of Sacramento County, 20 Sept. 2013. Web. 27 Sept. 2013. <http://www.sacdems.org/democratic-party-of-sacramento-county-calls-for-and-accepts-resignation-of-communications-chair/>.

Larson, Leslie. "California Democrat to Sen. Ted Cruz aide: I hope your kids 'die from debilitating, painful and incurable diseases' after vote against Obamacare." *New York Daily News* 20 Sept. 2013: n. pag. Daily News. Web. 27 Sept. 2013.

Bassett, Laura. "NRSC Tweets Sexualized Attack Against Alison Lundergan Grimes." The Huffington Post. TheHuffingtonPost.com, 19 Nov. 2013. Web. 24 Dec. 2013. <http://www.huffingtonpost.com/2013/11/19/alison-

lundergan-grimes-
obamagirl_n_4303766.html?utm_hp_ref=tw>.

Macneal, Caitlin. "TPMDayBreaker." Talking Points Memo. Talking Points Memo, 17 Dec. 2013. Web. 24 Dec. 2013. <http://talkingpointsmemo.com/livewire/poll-candidates-nearly-tied-in-kentucky-senate-race>.

Schultheis, Emily. "POLITICO." POLITICO. N.p., 19 Nov. 2013. Web. 27 Dec. 2013. <http://www.politico.com/story/2013/11/national-republican-senatorial-committee-obama-girl-tweet-alison-lundergan-grimes-kentucky-senate-election-2014-100078.html>.

"Election Results." Bangor Daily News. N.p., n.d. Web. 3 July 2014. <http://maineelections.bangordailynews.com/>

Machaud, Michael. "Mike Michaud: Yes, I am gay. But why should it matter?" *Bangor Daily News* 4 Nov. 2013: n. pag. BDN Maine Opinion. Web. 18 Dec. 2013.

"Maine Equal Rights Center." Maine Equal Rights Center RSS. N.p., n.d. Web. 14 Dec. 2013. <http://www.maineequalrightscenter.com/about/>.

Moretto, Mario. "State & Capitol." State & Capitol. Bangor Daily News, 16 Dec. 2013. Web. 18 Dec. 2013. <http://stateandcapitol.bangordailynews.com/2013/12/16/state-gop-rebukes-collins-primary-challenger-for-facebook-comments-about-michaudmandela/#.UsVix8aqmSq>.

Thistle, Scott. "Mike Michaud makes run for Maine governor official." *Bangor Daily News* 15 Aug. 2013: n. pag. BDN Maine Politics. Web. 18 Dec. 2013.

Esquith, Elias. "Florida state House candidate Joshua Black wants President Obama hanged for treason." Salon. N.p., 21 Jan. 2014. Web. 7 Feb. 2014. <http://www.salon.com/2014/01/21/florida_state_house_ca

ndidate_joshua_black_wants_president_obama_hanged_for
_treason/>.

Puente, Mark. "Florida House candidate Joshua Black calls
for hanging of President Obama." *Tampa Bay* 20 Jan. 2014:
1. Print.

Scott, Dylan. "TPMDayBreaker." Talking Points Memo. N.p.,
21 Jan. 2014. Web. 4 Feb. 2014.
<http://talkingpointsmemo.com/livewire/florida-gop-
candidate-obama-execution-secret-service>.

"Multi-County or District Offices." 2014 Florida Election
Watch -. N.p., n.d. Web. 6 Sept. 2014.
<http://enight.elections.myflorida.com/Offices/>.

Brooks, Jennifer. "Rep. Garofalo apologizes for tweet on NBA
that many called racist." *Star Tribune* [Minneapolis] 10 Mar.
2014: n. pag. StarTribune. Web. 2 Apr. 2013.

Kalaf, Samer. "This Man Is A State Representative
[UPDATE]." Deadspin. N.p., 9 Mar. 2014. Web. 3 Apr. 2014.
<http://deadspin.com/this-man-is-a-state-representative-
1540106215>.

Lapchick, Richard. "The 2013 Racial and Gender Report
Card: National Basketball Association." Tides. The Institute
for Diversity and Ethics in Sport, n.d. Web. 1 Apr. 2013.
<http://www.tidesport.org/RGRC/2013/2013_NBA_RGRC.pd
f>.

Grandoni, Dino. "Congressman Falls for The Onion's Planned
Parenthood 'Abortionplex' Story - The Wire." The Wire. N.p.,
6 Feb. 2012. Web. 7 Apr. 2014.
<http://www.thewire.com/national/2012/02/congressman-
falls-months-old-onion-story-about-planned-parenthood-
abortionplex/48344/>.

Grossman, Samantha. "Time.com." NewsFeed Louisiana
Congressman Mistakes Onion Story for Factual News
Comments. *Time Magazine*, 7 Feb. 2012. Web. 7 Apr. 2014.

<http://newsfeed.time.com/2012/02/07/louisiana-congressman-mistakes-the-onions-planned-parenthood-story-for-factual-news/>.

"National Right to Life - Rep. John Fleming (R-Louisiana) biography." National Right to Life. N.p., n.d. Web. 5 Apr. 2014. <http://nrlc.www.capwiz.com/bio/id/21024>.

"Planned Parenthood Opens $8 Billion Abortionplex | The Onion - America's Finest News Source." Planned Parenthood Opens $8 Billion Abortionplex | The Onion - America's Finest News Source. N.p., 18 May 2011. Web. 7 Apr. 2014. <http://www.theonion.com/articles/planned-parenthood-opens-8-billion-abortionplex,20476/>.

"KitchenAid apologizes for tweet about Obama grandmother." *USA Today* [Atlanta] 4 Oct. 2012: n. pag. USA Today. Web. 1 Oct. 2013.

Stenovec, Timothy. "KitchenAid Twitter Account Sends Offensive Tweet About Obama's Deceased Grandmother (TWEETS)." The Huffington Post. TheHuffingtonPost.com, 4 Oct. 2012. Web. 2 Oct. 2013. <http://www.huffingtonpost.com/2012/10/04/kitchen-aid-twitter-tweet-obamagrandmother_n_1938031.html>.

"The Analytics of a Twitter Nightmare: Dissecting the KitchenAid Tweet." Simply Measured Analytics Blog. N.p., n.d. Web. 1 Oct. 2013. <http://simplymeasured.com/blog/2012/10/04/kitchenaid-twitter-mistake-analytics/>.

White, Martha. "KitchenAid apologizes for dead grandma Obama debate Tweet." NBC News Business. NBC News, 4 Oct. 2012. Web. 2 Oct. 2013. <http://www.nbcnews.com/business/kitchenaid-apologizes-dead-grandma-obama-debate-tweet-6273754>.

"'AURORA' WHITE PLEATED V NECK STRONG SHOULDER DRESS - INSPIRED BY KIM KARDASHIAN." Celeb Boutique. N.p., n.d. Web. 4 Oct. 2013.

<http://www.celebboutique.com/index.php?dispatch=produ cts.view&product_id=1005>.

Haberman, Stephanie. "CelebBoutique Misguided Aurora Tweet Sparks Twitter Outrag." Mashable. N.p., 20 July 2012. Web. 6 Oct. 2013. <http://mashable.com/2012/07/20/celebboutique-misguided-aurora-tweet-sparks-twitter-outrage/>.

Long, Mary. "Should We Believe @CelebBoutique's #Aurora Tweet Explanation?." AllTwitter. N.p., 5 Oct. 2013. Web. 23 July 2013. <http://www.mediabistro.com/alltwitter/celebboutique_b25 798>.

"2011 Egyptian protests Death Toll." Wikipedia. Wikimedia Foundation, n.d. Web. 7 Oct. 2013. <http://en.wikipedia.org/wiki/Template:2011_Egyptian_prot ests_Death_Toll>.

Baker, Scott. "Liberal Fashion Designer Kenneth Cole Apologizes for Egypt Tweet." The Blaze. N.p., 4 Feb. 2011. Web. 8 Oct. 2013. <http://www.theblaze.com/stories/2011/02/04/liberal-fashion-designer-kenneth-cole-apologizes-for-egypt-tweet/>.

Bhasin, Kim. "Kenneth Cole: Offensive Tweets Are Simply Good Business Strategy." The Huffington Post. TheHuffingtonPost.com, 6 Sept. 2013. Web. 4 Oct. 2013. <http://www.huffingtonpost.com/2013/09/06/kenneth-cole-twitter_n_3881085.html>.

Bhasin, Kim. "Kenneth Cole: Offensive Tweets Are Simply Good Business Strategy." The Huffington Post. TheHuffingtonPost.com, 6 Sept. 2013. Web. 6 Oct. 2013. <http://www.huffingtonpost.com/2013/09/06/kenneth-cole-twitter_n_3881085.html>.

Farhi, Paul. "Bush Ads Using 9/11 Images Stir Anger."
Washington Post 5 Mar. 2004: n. pag. Washington Post.
Web. 7 Oct. 2013.

Lake, Chris. "Kenneth Cole uses social media to stir up
controversy." Econsultancy. N.p., 15 Aug. 2011. Web. 7 Oct.
2013. <http://econsultancy.com/us/blog/7886-kenneth-
cole-uses-social-media-to-stir-up-controversy>.

Crowell, Grant. "Rick Perry's Viral Video Disaster: What
Politicians Do Wrong On YouTube." ReelSEO. N.p., 10 Dec.
2011. Web. 8 Oct. 2013. <http://www.reelseo.com/rick-
perry-viral-video-stron/>.

"Daily Kos." Rick Perry 'Strong' More Dislikes On Youtube
Than Rebecca Black 'Friday'. N.p., 12 Dec. 2011. Web. 5
Oct. 2013.
<http://www.dailykos.com/story/2011/12/12/1044487/-
Rick-Perry-Strong-More-Dislikes-On-Youtube-Than-Rebecca-
Black-Friday#>.

Gibson, Megan. "Time NewsFeed." Rick Perry's Strong
Campaign Ad Gets the Web Angry and Laughing Comments.
Time, 9 Dec. 2011. Web. 7 Oct. 2013.
<http://newsfeed.time.com/2011/12/09/rick-perrys-strong-
campaign-ad-gets-the-web-angry-and-laughing/>.

Praetorius, Dean. "Rick Perry's 'Strong' Ad Surpasses
Rebecca Black's 'Friday' With More Dislikes On YouTube
(VIDEOS) [UPDATE]." The Huffington Post.
TheHuffingtonPost.com, 8 Dec. 2011. Web. 5 Oct. 2013.
<http://www.huffingtonpost.com/2011/12/08/rick-perry-
rebecca-black-youtube-dislikes_n_1138000.html>.

Stein, Sam. "Rick Perry's Anti-Gay Iowa Ad Divides His Top
Staff." The Huffington Post. TheHuffingtonPost.com, 8 Dec.
2011. Web. 7 Oct. 2013.
<http://www.huffingtonpost.com/2011/12/08/rick-perry-
anti-gay-iowa-ad-divides-top-staff_n_1136587.html>.

"Strong." YouTube. Rick Perry for President, 6 Dec. 2011. Web. 5 Oct. 2013. <http://www.youtube.com/watch?v=0PAJNntoRgA>.

Ward, Caroline. "Rick Perry 2012 Campaign for President: News and updates." Rick Perry's top ten opps moments of his campaign. N.p., 12 Jan. 2019. Web. 10 Sept. 2013. <http://blog.chron.com/rickperry/2012/01/rick-perry%E2%80%99s-top-tenoops-moments-of-his-campaign/>.

AFP. "Yokohama mistakenly tweets N Korean missile launch." ABC News Australia. N.p., 10 Apr. 2013. Web. 16 Sept. 2013. <http://www.abc.net.au/news/2013-04-10/japan-city-mistakenly-tweetsn-korean-missile-launch/4621456>.

Chen, Jason. "Just Where Can North Korea's Missiles Hit?." Gizmodo. Gizmodo, 9 June 1925. Web. 15 Sept. 2013. <http://gizmodo.com/5302604/just-where-can-north-koreas-missiles-hit>.

"Distance from Yokohama to north Korea." Distance Calculator. N.p., n.d. Web. 15 Sept. 2013. <http://www.timeanddate.com/worldclock/distances.html?n=667>.

"Japan city mistakenly tweets N. Korean missile launch." Rappler. N.p., 10 Apr. 2013. Web. 15 Sept. 2013. <http://www.rappler.com/world/25940-japan-city-mistakenly-tweets-n-korean-missile-launch>.

"Lessons Learned: Social Media and Hurricane Sandy." Department of Homeland Security. N.p., n.d. Web. 13 Sept. 2013. <http://www.naseo.org/Data/Sites/1/documents/committees/energysecurity/documents/dhs_vsmwg_lessons_learned_social_media_and_hurricane_sandy_formatted_june_2013_final.pdf>.

Reisinger, Don. "Yokohama misfires tweet about North Korea missile launch." CNET News. CBS Interactive, 10 Apr. 2013. Web. 14 Sept. 2013. <http://news.cnet.com/8301-1023_3-57578812-93/yokohama-misfires-tweet-about-north-korea-missile-launch/>.

AP. "Vatican's communications site runs Batman story." *USA Today* [Atlanta] 21 Mar. 2013: 1. USA Today. Web. 14 Oct. 2013.

Boone, John. "The Vatican Accidentally Tweets About Batman." E! Online. N.p., 22 Mar. 2013. Web. 15 Oct. 2013. <http://www.eonline.com/news/400482/the-vatican-accidentally-tweets-about-batman>.

"Holy smoke! Vatican tweets story about Batman... and it wasn't even a mistake." *Daily Mail* [London] 22 Mar. 2013: n. pag. Mail Online. Web. 15 Oct. 2013.

"Pope Francis Twitter Page." Twitter. Twitter, n.d. Web. 16 Oct. 2013. <https://twitter.com/Pontifex>.

RACHEL DONADIO, GAIA PIANIGIANI. "Twitter Has a New User: The Pope." *New York Times* 3 Dec. 2012: 1. New York Times. Web. 14 Oct. 2013.

Stegeman, John. "Twitter account @Pontifex has tweets deleted, Benedict XVI's coat of arms taken off Vatican website | Catholic Telegraph." Catholic Telegraph. N.p., n.d. Web. 15 Oct. 2013. <http://www.thecatholictelegraph.com/twitter-account-pontifex-has-tweets-deleted-benedict-xvis-coat-of-arms-taken-off-vatican-website/12828>.

"VaticanCommunication Twitter Page." Twitter. The Vatican, 21 Mar. 2013. Web. 15 Oct. 2013. <https://twitter.com/PCCS_VA/status/314771831137648641>.

Chorley, Matt. "Red-faced Conservative MP accidentally tweets link to a PORN website... but blames Tory HQ for his web blunder." *The Daily Mail* [London] 3 Apr. 2013: n. pag. Mail Online. Web. 20 Sept. 2013.

Mason, Rowena. "MP accidentally sends Twitter followers to 'porn website'." *The Telegraph* [London] 3 Apr. 2013: n. pag. The Telegraph. Web. 18 Oct. 2013.

"UK members of parliament." Deleted tweet from Rob Wilson (UKMPs). Politwoops UK, n.d. Web. 18 Oct. 2013. <http://www.politwoops.co.uk/p/ukmps/RobWilson_RDG/31 9385329104719872>.

ABC13 Evening News. ABC13. 19 Oct. 2010. Web. Transcript.

"How Jerry Brown got back in the governor's saddle." CNN Politics. CNN, 3 Nov. 2010. Web. 20 Oct. 2013. <http://news.blogs.cnn.com/2010/11/03/how-jerry-brown-got-back-in-the-governors-saddle/?hpt=C1>.

Malcolm, Andrew. "Top of the Ticket." Nearly a full day later, Meg Whitman's spokeswoman is still linking to cross-dressing Korean bass player. Los Angeles Times, 19 Oct. 2010. Web. 21 Oct. 2013. <http://latimesblogs.latimes.com/washington/2010/10/meg -whitman-bass-player.html>.

Matyszczyk, Chris. "Meg Whitman's campaign links to man in tutu." CNET News. CBS Interactive, 20 Oct. 2010. Web. 21 Oct. 2013. <http://news.cnet.com/8301-17852_3-20020170-71.html>.

"PolitiCal." Whitman campaign typo underscores the dangers of tweeting. Los Angeles Times, 18 Oct. 2010. Web. 21 Oct. 2013. <http://latimesblogs.latimes.com/california-politics/2010/10/whitman-campaign-typo-underscores-the-dangers-of-tweeting.html>.

"Suffolk Poll of California: Incumbent Boxer with 9 Point Lead for U.S. Senate." Suffolk University. Suffolk University,

n.d. Web. 22 Oct. 2013.
<http://www2.suffolk.edu/44241.html>.

Kopan, Tal. "Dan Pfeiffer sorry for 'N-word' gaffe."
POLITICO. N.p., 8 Oct. 2013. Web. 22 Oct. 2013.
<http://www.politico.com/story/2013/10/danpfeiffer-n-word-twitter-apology-97988.html>.

Alter, Charlotte. "Obamacare Approval Ratings Hit Record
Low Comments." Swampland. Time, 23 Dec. 2013. Web. 26
Dec. 2013.
<http://swampland.time.com/2013/12/23/obamacare-approval-ratings-hit-record-low/>.

Lavender, Paige. "White House Makes Twitter Typo,
Encourages People To Give Their Moms 'Piece Of Mind'." The
Huffington Post. TheHuffingtonPost.com, 13 Dec. 2013.
Web. 27 Dec. 2013.
<http://www.huffingtonpost.com/2013/12/13/white-house-twitter-typo_n_4441887.html?utm_hp_ref=politics>.

"Obama can't even spell right "Piece" of Mind?." Fire Andrea
Mitchell. N.p., n.d. Web. 26 Dec. 2013.
<http://www.fireandreamitchell.com/2013/12/12/obama-cant-even-spell-right-piece-mind/>.

"PolitiFact's "Lie Of The Year" Is One Of Fox's Favorite
Health Care Lies." Media Matters. N.p., 17 Dec. 2010. Web.
26 Dec. 2013.
<http://mediamatters.org/research/2010/12/17/politifactslie-of-the-year-is-one-of-foxs-favo/174497>.

"President's Obamacare photo becomes comical 'Obama
Holding a Sign' meme." New York Daily News 13 Dec. 2013:
n. pag. Daily News. Web. 27 Dec. 2013.

"White House #SpellingFail: Obamacare will "give your mom
piece of mind" " The Daily Caller. N.p., 12 Dec. 2013. Web.
26 Dec. 2013. <http://dailycaller.com/2013/12/12/white-house-spellingfail-obamacare-will-give-your-mom-piece-of-mind/>.

"White House Twitter Feed." Twitter. N.p., 12 Dec. 2013.
Web. 26 Dec. 2013.
<http://www.twitter.com/WhiteHouse>.

"AP Twitter feed hacked; no attack at White House." *USA Today* [Atlanta] 23 Apr. 2013: n. pag. USA Today. Web. 25 Oct. 2013.

Fisher, Max. "Syrian hackers claim AP hack that tipped stock market by $136 billion. Is it terrorism?." *The Washington Post* 23 Apr. 2013: n. pag. Washington Post. Web. 24 Oct. 2013.

Fung, Katherine. "Associated Press Twitter Account Restored After Hack." The Huffington Post. TheHuffingtonPost.com, 24 Apr. 2013. Web. 25 Oct. 2013.
<http://www.huffingtonpost.com/2013/04/24/associated-press-twitter-restored-hack_n_3147333.html>.

"Getting started with login verification | Twitter Blogs." Twitter Blogs. Twitter, 22 May 2013. Web. 26 Oct. 2013.
<https://blog.twitter.com/2013/getting-started-with-login-verification>.

"Hackers Compromise AP Twitter Account." The Big Story. Associated Press, 23 Apr. 2013. Web. 26 Oct. 2013.
<http://bigstory.ap.org/article/hackers-compromise-ap-twitter-account>.

JONATHAN CHENG, , MIKE CHERNEY and JERRY DICOLO. "Stocks Notch Strong Finish After Reeling From Fake Tweet." *The Wall Street Journal* [New York] 23 Apr. 2013: n. pag. The Wall Street Journal. Web. 24 Oct. 2013.

Perez, Sarah. "AP Twitter Hack Preceded By A Phishing Attempt, News Org Says." TechCrunch. N.p., 23 Apr. 2013. Web. 24 Oct. 2013.
<http://techcrunch.com/2013/04/23/ap-twitter-hack-preceded-by-a-phishing-attempt-news-org-says/>.

Rosa Golijan, Wilson Rothman. "Nbc News Technology." NBC News. N.p., 23 Apr. 2013. Web. 25 Oct. 2013. <http://www.nbcnews.com/technology/ap-twitter-account-hacked-posts-false-white-house-scare-6C9560165>.

Anderson, Chris. "Hurricane Sandy Power Outage Map: Millions Without Electricity On East Coast (INFOGRAPHIC)." The Huffington Post. TheHuffingtonPost.com, 30 Oct. 2012. Web. 28 Oct. 2013. <http://www.huffingtonpost.com/2012/10/30/hurricane-sandy-power-outagemap-infographic_n_2044411.html>.

Bello, Marisol. "Hurricane Sandy shows dark side of social media." USA Today [Atlanta] 31 Oct. 2012: n. pag. USA Today. Web. 29 Oct. 2013.

Kaczynski, Andrew. "BuzzFeed." BuzzFeed. N.p., 31 Oct. 2012. Web. 28 Oct. 2013. <http://www.buzzfeed.com/andrewkaczynski/councilman-pushes-for-charges-against-twitter-user>.

Leader, Jessica. "Superstorm Sandy Deaths, Damage And Magnitude: What We Know One Month Later." The Huffington Post. TheHuffingtonPost.com, 29 Nov. 2012. Web. 28 Oct. 2013. <http://www.huffingtonpost.com/2012/11/29/superstorm-hurricane-sandy-deaths-2012_n_2209217.html>.

"New York House Election Results." POLITICO. N.p., 19 Nov. 2012. Web. 29 Oct. 2013. <http://www.politico.com/2012-election/results/house/new-york/>.

Steuf, Jack. "BuzzFeed." BuzzFeed. N.p., 30 Oct. 2012. Web. 28 Oct. 2013. <http://www.buzzfeed.com/jackstuef/the-man-behind-comfortablysmug-hurricane-sandys>.

Gearan, Anne. "White House National Security Staffer Reportedly Fired for Twitter Postings under Alias; Jofi Joseph, a Nonproliferation Expert at the National Security Council, Was Fired Last Week." The Washington Post 23 Oct.

2013: n. pag. Washington Post - Politics. Web. 25 Oct. 2013.

Itkowitz, Colby. "Casey "stunned" former staffer was secret White House tweeter." The Morning Call [Allentown] 23 Oct. 2013: n. pag. The Morning Call - Pennsylvania Avenue. Web. 26 Oct. 2013.

"National Security Agency / Central Security Service - Top Banner." Hiring Requirements for the National Security Agency (NSA). NSA, n.d. Web. 25 Oct. 2013. <http://www.nsa.gov/careers/jobs_search_apply/hirerequir e.shtml>.

"National Security Agency / Central Security Service - Top Banner." The NSA/CSS Mission. NSA, n.d. Web. 25 Oct. 2013. <http://www.nsa.gov/about/mission/index.shtml>.

Rogin, Josh. "Exclusive: White House Official Fired for Tweeting Under Fake Name." The Daily Beast. Newsweek/Daily Beast, 22 Oct. 2013. Web. 25 Oct. 2013. <http://www.thedailybeast.com/articles/2013/10/22/white-house-official-fired-fortweeting-under-fake-name1.html>.

"Stung by a Twitter Renegade, Group in Obama Administration Launched Sting of Its Own (Posted 2013-10-24 16:38:38); before the Outing of @ Natsecwonk, the Group Planted False Information to See If the Tidbit Appeared Online." The Washington Post 24 Oct. 2013: n. pag. Washington Post - Politics. Web. 25 Oct. 2013.

Thrush, Glenn. "POLITICO." POLITICO. N.p., 22 Oct. 2013. Web. 25 Oct. 2013. <http://www.politico.com/politico44/2013/10/nsc-aide-admits-twitter-attack-on-white-house-175722.html>.

"First President on TV." Infoplease. Infoplease, n.d. Web. 16 Nov. 2013. <http://www.infoplease.com/askeds/first-president-tv.html>.

"Harding becomes first president to be heard on the radio." History.com. A&E Television Networks, n.d. Web. 16 Nov. 2013. <http://www.history.com/this-day-in-history/harding-becomes-first-president-to-be-heard-on-the-radio>.

O'Keefe, Kevin. "Almost 70% of 14-30 year-olds get their news from social media." Real Lawyers Have Blogs. N.p., 30 Mar. 2013. Web. 15 Nov. 2013. <http://kevin.lexblog.com/2013/05/30/almost-70-of-14-30-year-olds-get-their-news-from-social-media/>.

"Social Media - the 21st Century News Source." Social Media Today. N.p., 22 Mar. 2012. Web. 15 Nov. 2013. <http://socialmediatoday.com/dlawrence/475239/social-media-now-majo>